VRA 001 Elementary and Special Education Teachers
Teacher Certification Exam

By: Sharon Wynne, M.S.
Southern Connecticut State University

"And, while there's no reason yet to panic, I think it's only prudent that we make preparations to panic."

XAMonline, INC.
Boston

Library of Congress Cataloging-in-Publication Data

Wynne, Sharon A.
  VRA Elementary and Special Education Teachers: Teacher Certification/Sharon A. Wynne. -1st ed.
    ISBN 978-1-60787-109-5
    1. VRA 001   2. Study Guides.   3. Virginia
    4. Teachers' Certification & Licensure.   5. Careers

Disclaimer:

The opinions expressed in this publication are the sole works of XAMonline and were created independently from the National Education Association, Educational Testing Service, or any State Department of Education, National Evaluation Systems or other testing affiliates.

Between the time of publication and printing, state specific standards as well as testing formats and website information may change that is not included in part or in whole within this product. Sample test questions are developed by XAMonline and reflect similar content as on real tests; however, they are not former tests. XAMonline assembles content that aligns with state standards but makes no claims nor guarantees teacher candidates a passing score. Numerical scores are determined by testing companies such as NES or ETS and then are compared with individual state standards. A passing score varies from state to state.

Printed in the United States of America   œ-1

VRA 001: for Elementary and Special Education Teachers
ISBN: 978-1-60787-109-5

TABLE OF CONTENTS

Great Study and Testing Tips!

What to study in order to prepare for the subject assessments is the focus of this study guide but equally important is *how* you study.

You can increase your chances of truly mastering the information by taking some simple, but effective, steps.

Study Tips:

1. <u>Some foods aid the learning process</u>. Foods such as milk, nuts, seeds, rice, and oats help your study efforts by releasing natural memory enhancers called CCKs (*cholecystokinin*) composed of *tryptophan*, *choline*, and *phenylalanine*. All of these chemicals enhance the neurotransmitters associated with memory. Before studying, try a light, protein-rich meal of eggs, turkey, and fish. All of these foods release the memory enhancing chemicals. The better the connections, the more you comprehend.

Likewise, before you take a test, stick to a light snack of energy boosting and relaxing foods. A glass of milk, a piece of fruit, or some peanuts all release various memory-boosting chemicals and help you to relax and focus on the subject at hand.

2. <u>Learn to take great notes</u>. A by-product of our modern culture is that we have grown accustomed to getting our information in short doses (i.e. TV news sound bites or *USA Today* style newspaper articles.)

Consequently, we have subconsciously trained ourselves to assimilate information better in <u>neat little packages</u>. If your notes are scrawled all over the paper, it fragments the flow of the information. Strive for clarity. Newspapers use a standard format to achieve clarity. Your notes can be much clearer through use of proper formatting. A very effective format is called the <u>*"Cornell Method."*</u>

Take a sheet of loose-leaf lined notebook paper and draw a line all the way down the paper about 1-2" from the left-hand edge.

Draw another line across the width of the paper about 1-2" up from the bottom. Repeat this process on the reverse side of the page.

Look at the highly effective result. You have ample room for notes, a left hand margin for special emphasis items or inserting supplementary data from the textbook, a large area at the bottom for a brief summary, and a little rectangular space for just about anything you want.

3. Get the concept than the details. Too often, we focus on the details and do not gather an understanding of the concept. However, if you simply memorize only dates, places, or names, you may well miss the whole point of the subject.

A key way to understand things is to put them in your own words. If you are working from a textbook, automatically summarize each paragraph in your mind. If you are outlining text, do not simply copy the author's words.

Rephrase them in your own words. You remember your own thoughts and words much better than someone else's and subconsciously tend to associate the important details with the core concepts.

4. Ask Why? Pull apart written material paragraph by paragraph and do not forget the captions under the illustrations.

Example: If the heading is "Stream Erosion", flip it around to read "Why do streams erode?" Then answer the questions.

If you train your mind to think in a series of questions and answers, not only will you learn more, but it also helps to lessen the test anxiety because you are used to answering questions.

5. Read for reinforcement and future needs. Even if you only have ten minutes, put your notes or a book in your hand. Your mind is similar to a computer; you have to input data in order to have it processed. *By reading, you are creating the neural connections for future retrieval.* The more times you read something, the more you reinforce the learning of ideas.

Even if you do not fully understand something on the first pass, *your mind stores much of the material for later recall.*

6. Relax to learn, so go into exile. Our bodies respond to an inner clock called biorhythms. Burning the midnight oil works well for some people but not everyone.

If possible, set aside a particular place to study that is free of distractions. Shut off the television, cell phone, and pager and exile your friends and family during your study period.

If you really are bothered by silence, try background music. Light classical music at a low volume has been shown over other types to aid in concentration. Music without lyrics that evokes pleasant emotions is highly suggested. Try just about anything by Mozart. It relaxes you.

7. <u>**Use arrows not highlighters.**</u> At best, it is difficult to read a page full of yellow, pink, blue, and green streaks. Try staring at a neon sign for a while and you will soon see that the horde of colors obscures the message.

A quick note, a brief dash of color, an underline, or an arrow pointing to a particular passage is much clearer than a horde of highlighted words.

8. <u>**Budget your study time.**</u> Although you should not ignore any of the material, *allocate your available study time in the same ratio that topics may appear on the test.*

Testing Tips:

1. <u>Get smart; play dumb</u>. Don't read anything into the question. Do not assume that the test writer is looking for something else than what is asked. Stick to the question as written and do not read extra things into it.

2. <u>Read the question and all the choices *twice* before answering the question</u>. You may miss something by not carefully reading, and then re-reading, both the question and the answers.

If you really do not have a clue as to the right answer, leave it blank on the first time through. Go on to the other questions, as they may provide a clue as to how to answer the skipped questions.

If later on, you still cannot answer the skipped ones . . . *Guess.* The only penalty for guessing is that you *might* get it wrong. Only one thing is certain; if you don't put anything down, you will get it wrong!

3. <u>Turn the question into a statement</u>. Look at the way the questions are worded. The syntax of the question usually provides a clue. Does it seem more familiar as a statement rather than as a question? Does it sound strange?

By turning a question into a statement, you may be able to spot if an answer sounds right, and it may also trigger memories of material you have read.

4. <u>Look for hidden clues</u>. It is actually very difficult to compose multiple-foil (choice) questions without giving away part of the answer in the options presented.

In most multiple-choice questions you can often readily eliminate one or two of the potential answers. This leaves you with only two real possibilities and automatically your odds go to fifty-fifty for very little work.

5. <u>Trust your instincts</u>. For every fact that you have read, you subconsciously retain something of that knowledge. On questions that you are not certain about, go with your basic instincts. **Your first impression on how to answer a question is usually correct.**

6. <u>Mark your answers directly on the test booklet</u>. Do not bother trying to fill in the optical scan sheet on the first pass through the test.

Just be very careful not to mis-mark your answers when you eventually transcribe them to the scan sheet.

7. <u>Watch the clock</u>! You have a set amount of time to answer the questions. Do not get bogged down trying to answer a single question at the expense of ten questions you can more readily answer.

DOMAIN I. ASSESSMENT AND DIAGNOSTIC TEACHING

0001 **Understand the characteristics and uses of assessment and screening measures for evaluating students' language proficiency and reading skills.**

Criterion-Referenced Tests

Criterion-referenced tests measure children's reading achievement against criteria or guidelines which are uniform for all the test takers. Therefore, by definition, no special questions, formats, or considerations are made for the test taker who is either from a different linguistic/cultural background or is already identified as a struggling reader/writer. On a criterion-referenced test, it is possible that a child test taker can score 100% because the child may have actually been exposed to all of the concepts taught and has mastered them. A child's score on such a test would indicate which of the concepts have already been taught and what additional review or support is needed to master the concept.

Two criterion-referenced tests that are commonly used to assess children's reading achievement are the Diagnostic Indicators of Basic Early Literacy Skills (DIBELS) and the Stanford Achievement Test. DIBELS measures progress in literacy from kindergarten to grade three. It can be downloaded from the Internet free at dibels.uoregon.edu. The Stanford is designed to measure individual children's achievement in key school subjects. Subtests covering various reading skills are part of this test. Both DIBELS and the Stanford Achievement Test are group-administered.

CTPIII

This criterion-referenced test measures verbal and quantitative ability in grades 3–12. It is targeted to help differentiate among the most capable students, i.e. those who rank above the 80th percentile on other standardized tests. This is a test that emphasizes higher order thinking skills and process-related reading comprehension questions.

Degrees of Reading Power (DRP)

This test is targeted to assess how well children understand the meaning of written text in real life situations. This test is supposed to measure the process of children's reading, not the products of reading such as identifying the main idea and author's purpose.

Norm-referenced Test

This test measures children against one another. Scores on this test are reported in percentiles. Each percentile indicates the percent of the testing population whose scores were lower than or the same as a particular child's score. Percentile is defined as a score on a scale of 100 showing the percentage of a distribution that is equal to or below it. This type of state-standardized norm-referenced test is being used in most districts today in response to the *No Child Left Behind Act.* While this type of test does not help tract the individual reader's progress in his or her ongoing reading development, it does permit comparisons across groups.

There are many more standardized norm-referenced tests to assess children's reading than there are criterion-referenced. In norm-referenced tests, scores are based on how well a child does compared to others, usually on the local, state, and national level. If the norming groups on the tests are reflective of the children being tested (e.g., same spread of minority, low income, and gifted students), the results are more trustworthy.

One of the best-known norm-referenced tests is the Iowa Test of Basic Skills. It assesses student achievement in various school subjects and has several subtests in reading. Other examples of norm-referenced tests used around the country are the Metropolitan Achievement Tests, the Terra Nova-2, and the Stanford Diagnostic Reading Test-4. These are all group tests. The Woodcock Reading Mastery test is an individual test that reading specialists use with students.

Concepts of Validity, Reliability, and Bias in Testing

Validity is how well a test measures what it is supposed to measure. Teacher-made tests are therefore not generally extremely valid, although they may be appropriate and valid in measuring of the specific concept the teacher wants to assess for his/her own children's achievement.

Reliability is the consistency of the test. This is measured by whether the test will indicate the same score for the child who takes it more than once.

Bias in testing occurs when the information within the test or the information required to be able to respond to a multiple-choice question or constructed response (essay question on the test) is information that is not available to some test takers who come from a different cultural, ethnic, linguistic, or socio-economic background than do the majority of the test takers. Since they have not had the same prior linguistic, social, or cultural experiences that the majority of test takers have had, these test takers are at a disadvantage in taking the test. No matter what their actual mastery of the material taught by the teacher, they may have difficulty addressing the "biased" questions. Generally other "non-biased" questions are given to them and eventually the biased questions are removed from the examination.

To solidify what might be abstract to the reader, on a recent reading test in one school system, the grade four reading comprehension multiple choice had some questions about the well-known fairy tale of *The Gingerbread Boy.* These questions were simple and accessible for most of the children in the class. But two children were recent arrivals from the Dominican Republic where they had learned English. Although they were reading on fourth-grade level, the story of *The Gingerbread Boy* was not read in their Dominican grade school. Therefore, a question about this story on the standardized reading test *did* demonstrate examiner bias and was not fair to these test takers.

Informal Assessments

Running Records
A running record of children's oral reading progress in the early grades K–3 is a pivotal informal assessment. It supports the teacher in deciding whether a book a child is reading is matched to his/her stage of reading development. In addition this assessment allows the teacher to analyze a child's miscues to see which cueing systems and strategies the child uses and to determine which other systems the child might use more effectively. Finally the running record offers a graphic account of a child's oral reading.

Generally, a teacher should maintain an annotated class notebook with pages set aside for all the children or individual notebooks for each child. One of the benefits of using running records as an informal assessment is that they can be used with any text and can serve as a tool for teaching, rather than an instrument to report on children's status in class.

Running records are meant to be updated frequently by the teacher so that the educator can truly observe a pattern of errors and provides the educator with sufficient information to analyze the child's reading progress over time. As any mathematician or scientist knows, the more samples of a process you gather over time, the more likely the teacher is to get an accurate picture of the child's reading needs.

Using the notations Marie Clay developed and shared in *An Observation Study of Early Literacy Achievement,* Sharon Taberski offers in her book, *On Solid Ground*, a lengthy walk through keeping a running record of children's reading. Taberski writes in the child's miscue on the top line of her running record above the text word. Indeed she records all of the child's miscue attempts on the line above the text word. Taberski advises the teacher to make all the miscue notations as the child reads, since this allows the teacher to get additional information about how and why the child makes miscue choices. Additionally, the teacher should note all self-corrections (coded SC) made when the child is monitoring his/her own reading, crosschecks information, and uses additional information.

As part of the informal assessment of primary grade reading, it is important to record the child's word insertions, omissions, requests for help, and attempts to get the word. In informal assessment the rate of accuracy can be estimated by dividing the child's errors by the total words read.

Results of a running record assessment can be used to select the best setting for the child's reading. If a child reads from 95%–100% correct, the child is ready for independent reading. If the child reads from 92%–97% right, the child is ready for guided reading. Below 92% the child needs a read-aloud or shared reading activity. Note that these percentages are slightly different from those one would use to match books to readers.

Literacy Portfolios

Compiling literacy portfolios is an increasingly popular and meaningful form of informal assessment. It is particularly compelling because artists, television directors, authors, architects, and photographers use portfolios in their careers and jobs. It is also a most authentic format for documenting children's literacy growth over time. The portfolio is not only a significant professional informal assessment tool for the teacher, but a vehicle and format for the child reader to take ownership of his/her progress over time. It models a way of compiling one's reading and writing products as a lifelong learner, which is the ultimate goal of reading instruction.

Portfolios can include the following four categories of materials:

- *Work Samples:* These can include children's story maps, webs, KWL charts, pictures, illustrations, storyboards, and writings about the stories they have read.
- *Records of Independent Reading and Writing:* These can include the children's journals, notebooks, or logs of books read with the names of the authors, titles of the books, date completed, and pieces related to books completed or in progress.

- *Checklists and Surveys:* These include checklists designed by the teacher for reading development, writing development, ownership checklists, and general interest surveys.

- *Self-Evaluation Forms:* These are the children's own evaluations of their reading and writing process framed in their own words. They can be simple templates with starting sentences such as:
    - I am really proud of the way I _____.
    - I feel one of my strengths as a reader is _____.
    - To improve the way I read aloud I need to _____.
    - To improve my reading I should _____.

Generally, child's portfolio in Grade 3 or above begins with a letter to the reader explaining the work that will be found in the portfolio. In Grade 4 and up, children write a brief reflection detailing their feelings and judgments about their growth as readers and writers.

When teachers maintain student portfolios for mandated school administrative review, district review, or even for their own research, they often prepare portfolio summary sheets. These provide identifying data on the children and then a timeline of their review of the portfolio contents. The summary sheets also contain professional comments on the extent to which the portfolio documents satisfactory and ongoing growth in reading.

Portfolios can be used beneficially for child-teacher and parent/teacher conversations to review the child's progress, discuss areas of strength, set future goals, make plans for future learning activities, and evaluate what should remain in the portfolio and what needs to be cleared out for new materials.

Rubrics

Holistic scoring involves assessing a child's ability to construct meaning through writing. It uses a scale called a *Rubric* usually ranges can range from 0 to 4:

> 0—Indicates the piece cannot be scored. It does not respond to the topic or is illegible.

> 1—The writing responds to the topic but does not cover it accurately.

> 2—The writing responds to the topic but lacks sufficient details or elaboration.

> 3—This piece fulfills the purpose of the writing assignment and has sufficient development (which refers to details, examples, and elaboration of ideas).

> 4—This response has the most details, best organization, and presents a well expressed reaction to the original writer's piece.

Miscue Analysis

This is a procedure that allows the teacher a look at the reading process. By definition, the miscue is an oral response different from the text being read. Sometimes miscues are also called unexpected responses or errors. By studying a student's miscues from an oral reading sample, the teacher can determine which cues and strategies the student is correctly using or not using in constructing meaning. Of course, the teacher can customize instruction to meet the needs of this particular student.

Informal Reading Inventories (IRI)

These are a series of samples of texts prearranged in stages of increasing difficulty. Listening to children read through these inventories, the teacher can pinpoint their skill level and the additional concepts they need to work on.

Characteristics and uses of Group versus Individual Reading Assessments

In assessment, tests are used for different purposes. They have different dimensions or characteristics whether they are given individually or in a group and whether they are standardized or teacher-made. The chart below shows the relationships of these elements.

	Standardized	**Teacher-made**
Individual	*Characteristics* • is uniformly administered *Uses* • is best for younger children • helps with placement for special services	*Characteristics* • has more flexibility *Uses* • assists teaching decisions • used for diagnostic purposes
Group	*Characteristics* • is uniformly administered • is time efficient *Uses* • permits comparisons across groups • used for policy decisions by administrators	*Characteristics* • has high face validity • is time efficient *Uses* • informs teach-reteach and enrichment decisions • documents students' learning

Techniques for Assessing Particular Reading Skills

Sharon Taberski recommends that the teacher build in one-on-one time for supporting individual children as needed in considering what makes sense, sounds right, and matches the letters. She notes that emergent and early readers tend to focus on meaning without adequate attention to graphophonic cues. She suggests using the following prompts for children who are having problems with graphophonic cues:

- Does what you said match the letters?

- If the word you said were _____, what letter would it have to start with?

- Look carefully at the first letters. Then, look at the middle letters. Then, look at the last letters. What could it be?

- If it word were _____, what letter or letters would it end with?

Oral retellings can be used to test children's comprehension. Children who are retelling a story to be tested for comprehension should be told that that is the purpose when they sit down with the teacher.

It is a good idea to let the child start the retelling on his/her own, because then the teacher can see whether he/she needs prompts to retell the story. Many times, more experienced readers summarize what they have read. This summary usually flows out along with the characters, the problem of the story, and other details.

Other signs that children understand what they are reading when they give an oral retelling include:

- Their use of illustrations to support the retelling

- References to the exact text in the retelling

- Emotional reaction to the text

- Making connections between the text and other stories or the readers' own experiences

- Giving information about the text without the teacher's asking for it

Responding to literature is one of the most important parts of reading. By the responses students give to what they have read, teachers can determine the level of comprehension. It takes practice for students to be able to respond critically to a text because they have the idea that all published authors are perfect and they should not criticize what they write.

Some of the strategies teachers can use to provide opportunities for students to give creative and personal responses to their reading include:

1. Reading Conferences—Ask a student to read a section of the text and then explain to you why he/she chose that section. Teachers can also ask students why they are reading a certain book or ask about their favorite author.

2. Reading Surveys—Teachers can devise a list of questions to find out what students are reading, how they decide what books to read, and how students feel about the topics or language used in the book.

3. Daily Reading Time—This could be a set time when everyone in the class, including the teacher, is reading, or it could be a center activity for a small group of children.

4. Literature Circles—Using the role sheets developed by Harvey Daniels in Voice and Choice in a Student-Centered Classroom, students take on different roles each day. They discuss the chapter or book, find new vocabulary words, illustrate a scene or pose questions for the group.

5. Reader's Theatre—Students adapt part of the book or story and make it into a choral reading with expression that shows how they felt about what they have read.

Responding to literature does not always take the form of written responses. In a Reader's Workshop, students can choose to respond to what they read by using art, painting, song, dance or any number of ways that serve as an interpretation of the reading. Interviewing the author or asking students to change a scene so the result is different are other examples of how students can give a personal response to reading.

Students who have a hard time coming up with a response would benefit from a sheet listing ideas for ways they can respond. These ideas usually take the form of open-ended sentences such as:

1. The character I liked the best was _____.

2. The character that is most like me is _____.

3. If I were _____, I would have _____

0002   Understand the use of assessment data to plan reading instruction.

Assessment is the practice of collecting information about children's progress, and evaluation is the process of judging the children's responses to determine how well they are achieving particular goals or demonstrating reading skills.

Assessment and evaluation are intricately connected in the literacy classroom. Assessment is necessary because teachers need ways to determine what students are learning and how they are progressing. In addition, assessment can be a tool that helps students take ownership of their own learning and become partners with their teachers and parents in their ongoing development as readers and writers. In this day of public accountability, clear, definite, and reliable assessment creates confidence in public education.

There are two broad categories of assessment. *Informal assessment* utilizes observations and other non-standardized procedures to compile anecdotal and observation data/evidence of children's progress. It includes but is not limited to checklists, observations, and performance tasks. *Formal assessment* is composed of standardized tests and procedures carried out under circumscribed conditions. Formal assessments include: state tests, standardized achievement tests, NAEP tests, and the like.

Effective Assessment Characteristics

1. It should be an *ongoing process* with the teacher making informal or formal assessments on an ongoing basis. The assessment should be a natural part of the instruction and not intrusive.

2. The most effective assessment is *integrated into ongoing instruction.* Throughout the teaching and learning day, the child's written, spoken, and reading contributions to the class or lack thereof, need to and can be continually noted.

3. Assessment should *reflect the child's actual reading and writing experiences.* The child should be able to show that he/she can read and explain or react to a similar literary or expository work.

4. Assessment needs to be a *collaborative and reflective process.* Teachers can learn from what the children reveal about their own individual assessments. Children, even as early as grade two, should be supported by their teacher to continually and routinely ask themselves questions assessing their reading. They might ask:
   a. "Do I understand what the author wants to say?"
   b. "What can I do to improve my reading?"
   c. "How can I use what I have read to learn more about this topic?"

   Teachers need to be informed by their own professional observation *and* by children's comments as they assess and customize instruction for children.

5. Quality assessment is *multidimensional* and may include but not be limited to samples of writings, student retellings, running records, anecdotal teacher observations, self-evaluations, and records of independent reading. From this multidimensional data, the teacher can derive a consistent level of performance and design additional instruction that will enhance the child's reading performance.

6. Assessment must *take into account children's age and ethnic/cultural patterns of learning.*

7. Effective assessment *teaches children from their strengths, not their weaknesses.* Find out what reading behaviors children demonstrate well and then design instruction to support those behaviors.

8. Assessment should be *part of children's learning process* and not done *to* them, but rather done *with* them.

Awareness of Text Leveling

The classroom library, in the context of the Balanced Literacy Approach to reading instruction, is focused on leveled books. These books have been leveled with the support of Fountas and Pinnell's *Guided Reading: Good First Teaching for All Children* and *Matching Books to Readers: Using Leveled Reading in Guided Reading, K–3.*

The books are leveled according to the designations in these reference books and need to be stored in bins or crates with front covers facing out. This makes them much easier for the children to identify. In that way the children can go through the appropriate levels and find those books of particular interest to them while staying in the level that is right for them to read. These are books that the children can read with the right degree of reading accuracy. When young children can see the cover of a book, they are more likely to flip through the book until they can independently identify an appealing book. Then they will read a little bit of the book to see if it's "just right."

"Just right" leveled books—books that children can read on their own—need to be available for them to read during independent reading. The goal is for the more fluent readers to select books on their own. Ultimately, the use of leveled books helps the children, in addition to the teacher, to decide which books are "good" or "just right" for them.

Levels are indicated by means color-coded stickers. A blue, yellow, red, or green dot sticker is placed in the upper right corner of each book to indicate emergent, early, transitional, and fluent reading stages, respectively. The books are then kept in containers with other "blue," "yellow," "red," and "green" books.

Other lists and resources other than Fountas and Pinnell which can be used to match children with "just right" books include the Reading Recovery level list. Ultimately, the teacher has to individualize whatever leveling is used in the library to address the individual learner's needs.

Awareness of the Challenges and Supports in a Text

Illustrations can be key supports for emergent and early readers. Teachers should not only use wordless stories (books which tell their narratives through pictures alone), but can also make targeted use of Big Books for read-alouds, so that young children become habituated to the use of illustrations as an important component for constructing meaning. The teacher should model for the child how to reference an illustration for help in identifying a word in the text the child does not recognize. Of course, children can also go on a picture walk with the teacher as part of a mini-lesson or guided reading and anticipate the story (narrative) using the pictures alone to construct meaning.

Decodability

Use literature that contains examples of letter sound correspondences you wish to teach. First, read the literature with the children or read it aloud to them. Then take a specific example from the text and have the children reread it as the teacher points out the letter-sound correspondence to the children. Then ask the children to go through the now-familiar literature to find other letter-sound correspondences. Once the children have correctly made the letter-sound correspondences, have them share similar correspondences they find in other works of literature

Cooper (2004) suggests that children can become word detectives so that they can independently and fluently decode on their own. The child should learn the following *word detective routines* so that he/she can function as an independent fluent reader who can decode words on his/her own:

- First the child should read to the end of a sentence.

- Then the child should search for word parts which he/she knows.

- The child should also try to decode the word from the letter sounds.

- As a last resort, the child should ask someone for help or look up the word in the dictionary.

Assessment of the Reading Development of Individual Students

For young readers who are from ELL backgrounds, even if they have been born in the United States, the use of pictures validates their story-authoring and storytelling skills and provides them with access and equity to the literary discussion and book talk of their native English-speaking peers. These children can also demonstrate their storytelling abilities by drawing sequels or prequels to the story detailed in the illustrations alone. They might even be given the opportunity to share the story aloud in their native language or to comment on the illustrations in their native language.

Since many stories today are recorded in two or even three languages at once, discussing story events or analyzing pictures in a different language is a beneficial practice that can be accomplished in the 21st century classroom. Use of pictures and illustrations can also help the K–3 educator assess the capabilities of children who are struggling readers if the children's learning strength is spatial. Through targeted questions about how the pictures would change if different plot twists occurred or how the child might transform the story through changing the illustrations, the teacher can begin to assess struggling reader's deficits and strengths.

Children from ELL backgrounds can benefit from listening to a recorded version of a particular story with which they can read along. This gives them another opportunity to "hear" the story correctly pronounced and presented and to begin to internalize its language structures. In the absence of taped versions of some key stories or texts, teachers may want to make their own sound recordings.

Highly proficient readers can also be involved in creating these literature recordings for use with ELL peers or younger peers. This of course develops oral language proficiency and also introduces these skilled readers into the intricacies of supporting ELL reading instruction. When they actually see their tapes being used by children, they will be tremendously gratified.

When using running records to informally assess the progress a student is making with their reading skills, it is important to note the types of errors the child is making. By examining the strategies and errors the student makes, the teacher can plan instruction, monitor progress, and assess skill levels. Even if not using a running record, teachers can use even more informal methods of using the errors a student makes to find significant ways to help the student improve in their reading.

Miscue analysis can be multi-faceted and provide both the teacher and reader with a wealth of important information. First, examining the methods a student uses to figure out unknown words helps the teacher understand which methods require further instruction or fine tuning and which have already been mastered. Typically, students use phonics skills (letter-sound correspondence), contextual clues (the other words in the sentence/passage), semantic analysis, or structural-analysis techniques to solve problems in reading. It is not through using only one of these methods that a reader becomes more proficient, but rather by using a combination of all of the approaches.

After collecting the running record, teachers can go back and look at which of the described strategies the students are successfully using. Tallying is one method to use. In this way, the educator can see the strategies used by the student and if one seems to be more dominant than others. This method will also help to point out specific strategies which are very weak for the student and would require more instruction. After this analysis, the teacher can develop an instructional plan to address weak areas and determine a more balanced problem-solving approach for the student.

Additionally, the teacher can look at the student's ability to monitor his/her own reading and comprehension. Noting these self-monitoring attempts allows the teacher to see if the student recognizes when they make a mistake. This is a very important skill for readers to develop. Once they realize something does not make sense, students should be able to go back and apply a correction strategy so as to not hinder comprehension. This becomes more important as the complexity of text increases.

Self-corrections by students begin to show a maturity of reading skills. However, students who make a tremendous amount of self-corrections lack fluency in reading and will eventually lose some comprehension. It is an important step for beginner readers, but as with any other learning process, we want students to pass through it rapidly, leaving in its place fluent, well-comprehended reading.

Adjustment of Reading Instruction Based on Ongoing Assessment

Running records of their students help teachers identify the cueing systems the children might be using. It is important for the teacher to adjust reading instruction based on the pattern of miscues gathered from several successive reading records. When the teacher carefully reviews a given student's substitutions and self-corrections, certain patterns begin to surface. For example, a child may use visual cues as he/she reads and adds meaning to self-correct. To the alert teacher, this reliance on visual miscues indicates that the reader doesn't make sense of what is being read. This means that the teacher needs to check what cueing system the child uses when he/she is reading "just right" books. Children who use meaning and structure but not visual/graphophonic cues need to be reminded and facilitated to understand the importance of getting and reconstructing the author's message. They have to be able to share the author's story, not their own.

Materials in a child's ongoing assessment notebook can not only be used by the teacher to adjust the child's current instruction, they can document for the child his/her growth as a successful reader over time. In addition, if the same concerns surface over the use of a particular cueing system or high frequency word, the teacher can adjust the class wall chart and even devote a whole class lesson to the particular element.

Techniques for Determining Students' Independent, Instructional, and Frustration Reading Levels

Instructional reading is generally judged to be at the 95% accuracy level, although Taberski places it at between 92% and 97%. Taberski tries to enhance the independent reading levels by making sure that readers on the instructional reading levels read a variety of genres, and have a range of available and interesting books within a particular genre to read.

Taberski's availability for reading conferences helps her to both assess first hand her children's frustration levels and to model ongoing teacher/reader book conversations by scheduling child-initiated reading conferences when she personally replenishes their book bags.

To allay children's frustration levels while reading and to foster their independent reading, it is important to some children that the teacher personally take time out to hear them read aloud and to check for fluency and expression. After they have read aloud, children's frustration level can be immeasurably lessened if they are explicitly told by the teacher that they need to read without pointing and that they should try chunking words into phrases that mimic their natural speech.

Strategies for Selecting and Using Meaningful Reading Materials at Appropriate Levels of Difficulty

Matching young children with "just right" books fosters their independent reading, no matter what their age. The teacher needs to have an extensive classroom library. Emergent readers and early readers should be matched with books that are set in fairly large print and have appropriate spacing to allow the reader to easily see where a word begins and ends. These books should have few words per page so that the young reader can focus on the all-important concerns of top-to-bottom, left-to-right, directionality, and the one-to-one match of word to print.

Illustrations for young children should support the meaning of the text and language patterns and predictable text structures should make these texts appealing to young readers. Most important, the content of the story should relate to the children's interests and experiences as the teacher knows them. Only after all these considerations have been addressed, can the teacher select "just right" books from an already leveled bin or list. Similarly, when the teacher is selecting books for transitional and fluent readers, the following ideas need to be taken into account:

Book Length
The book should take at least two sittings to complete, allowing children to get used to reading longer books.

Character Complexity and Plot Intricacy
The fluent and transitional reader needs to deal with more complex characters and more intricate plotting. Look for books that set the stage for plot development with a compelling beginning. Age appropriateness of the concepts, plot, and themes are important so that the child will sustain interest in the book.

Advanced Book Features
Look for book features such as Table of Contents or Index to help children navigate through the book. Series books are wonderful to introduce at this point in the children's development.

When considering both formal and informal assessment data gathered on students, it is important to quantify the information into terms easily recognized by other teachers, administrators, and parents. In reading, general practice is to categorize the information into levels of reading. These levels go across both kinds of assessments, using the percentage of word accuracy and comprehension to determine the reading level.

Levels of Reading

Independent
This is the level at which the child can read text totally on their own. When reading books at the independent level, students will be able to decode between 95%–100% of the words and comprehend the text at a level of 90% accuracy or better. Many bodies of research indicate that about 98% accuracy makes for a good independent reader; however, there is other research that goes as low as 95% accuracy.

Instructional
This is the level at which the student should be taught because it provides enough difficulty to increase their reading skills without providing so much that it becomes too cumbersome to finish the selection. Typically, the acceptable range for accuracy is between 85%–94% with 75% or greater comprehension. Some standards rely on the number of errors made instead of the accuracy percentage with no more than one error out of twenty words read being the acceptable standard.

Frustrational
Books at a student's frustrational level are too difficult for that child and should not be used. The frustrational level is any text with less than 85% word accuracy and/or less than 75% comprehension.

The use of independent, instructional, and frustrational levels allow educators to provide children with texts of different ranges depending on the skills necessary to be completed. Typically, standardized or formal assessments test to the instructional level. Therefore, if reading a standardized assessment such as an Iowa Test of Basic Skills, the reported reading level would be the instructional level for that student.

Additionally, some formal and informal test results use alternate methods of reporting information. Some use the grade level and month equivalent, where a 3.2 reading level would indicate the child is reading at the third grade level second month (typically October). Still others use their own leveling system. The Developing Readers Assessment (DRA) has its own unique method of coding book levels based on the work of Fountas and Pinnell. Regardless of the levels listed, the work can easily be translated into independent, instructional, and frustrational levels, by examining the comprehension and the word reading accuracy portions of the assessment.

DOMAIN II. ORAL LANGUANGE AND ORAL COMMUNICATION

0003 **Understand the development of oral language and oral communication skills.**

Language Acquisition

This is continuous and never-ending. From the perspective of this theory and research, all children come to school with a language base upon which the school must build. Since oral language and reading are connected, it is important that schools build literacy experiences around the language the child brings to the school.

Children from families where English is not spoken may lack a solid understanding of its syntactic and visual structure. Therefore, as they are being recorded for progress using the oral running record, they may need additional support from their teacher and from an English Language reading specialist in examining the structure and meaning of English. Children from a non-native English Language speaking background may often pronounce words that make no sense to them and just go on reading. They have to learn to stop to construct meaning and may have to be prompted to self-correct.

Children from non-native English Language speaking backgrounds can benefit from independent reading opportunities to listen to a familiar story on tape and read along. This also gives them practice in listening to standard English oral reading. Often these children can begin to internalize the language structures by listening to the book on tape several times.

Highly proficient readers can sometimes support early readers through a partner relationship. Some children, particularly the emergent and beginning early readers, benefit from reading books with partners. The partners sit side by side and each one takes turns reading the entire text.

Audio books and author web resources provides special needs learners—those with visual or auditory handicapping conditions—with immediate contact with authors and direct sharing in the joy of storytelling. In addition to the accessibility of the keyboard, their responses to literature can be shared with a broad network of other readers, including close peers and distant peers. Technology literally enfranchises special needs learners into the circle of connected readers and writers.

Reading, writing, listening, and speaking are the four main components of language arts at any grade level. They are interrelated and they complement each other. By ensuring that all four of these strands are woven into your language arts classes, you can ensure that you provide a balance of experiences to give students the instruction and support they need. With such a balance, the students are able to integrate all of the English language processes and build on their prior knowledge and experiences.

Speaking and listening may be viewed as separate from reading and writing, but all four form the main communication system of the English language. They are *interdependent*. All other forms of communication depend on the ability to speak and listen. They are also the foundation for many other language skills, which is why teachers should provide ample opportunities for students to speak and listen in class as part of the daily routine. Classrooms are places where talk flows freely. By taking advantage of this talk to find out where students are in their thinking about topics, themes, and responses to literature, teachers can easily assess this component of language arts. When students can express ideas in their own words, it helps them to make meaning of their experiences with reading.

Although students don't have a lot of problems with speaking in class, listening often must be nurtured and taught. Good listeners will respond emotionally, imaginatively, and intellectually to what they hear. Students need to be taught how to respond to presentations by their classmates in ways that are not harmful or derogatory in any way. There are also different types of listening that the teacher can develop in the students:

- Appreciative listening to enjoy an experience
- Attentive listening to gain knowledge
- Critical listening to evaluate arguments and ideas

Within the classroom setting, many opportunities will present themselves for students to speak and listen for various purposes and often these may be spontaneous. Activities for speaking and listening should be integrated throughout the language arts program, but there should also be times when speaking and listening are the focus of the instruction. By incorporating speaking and listening into the language arts program, students will begin to see the connection between the two and thus improve their reading skills more efficiently.

Some of the ways that speaking and listening can be integrated include:

- Conversations
- Small group discussions
- Brainstorming
- Interviewing
- Oral reading
- Readers' theater
- Choral speaking
- Storytelling
- Role playing
- Book talks
- Oral reports
- Class debates
- Listening to guest speakers

Reading and writing are two interrelated aspects of language development. Students will read print and then realize that they can convey similar messages by using written language. The connections to the generally more formal language in reading and the same type of language the students will be asked to produce in writing are plentiful. Students can begin to draw phrases from text and the conventions of written language from reading before they are able to apply those same strategies in writing. By combining the two, and explicitly showing students these connections, teachers can develop both skills more rapidly.

Strategies for Promoting Awareness of the Relationship between Spoken and Written Language

- The teacher writes down what the children are saying on a chart.

- Highlight and celebrate the meanings, uses, and print products found in the classroom. These products include: posters, labels, yellow sticky pad notes, labels on shelves and lockers, calendars, rule signs, and directions.

- The intentional reading of big-print and oversized books to teach print conventions[G1] such as directionality.

- Practice exercises in reading to others (for grades K, 1, and 2) where young children[G2] practice how to handle a book, how to turn pages, how to find tops and bottoms of pages, and how to tell the difference between the front and back covers of a book.

- Have children match oral words to printed words by forming an echo chorus as the teacher reads the story aloud. They echo the reading. Often this works best with poetry or rhymes.
- Have the children combine, manipulate, switch, and move letters to change words and spelling patterns.

- Work with letter cards to create messages and respond to the messages that they create.

Search and discuss adventures in word awareness and close observation where children are challenged to identify and talk about the length, appearance, and boundaries of specific words.

Developing the writing skills of students is a complex process. As with any other aspect of teaching, it's important to provide as many realistic opportunities as possible. When students read for an authentic purpose, the reading becomes more important and there is an increased interest in completing the task. The same is true of writing.

In writing, teachers often spend time having the students complete journals, write stories, or complete other assignments. While all of these types of writing provide skill development and can be important to complete with students, it is when you can find ways to incorporate authentic and relevant writing that students can find the same increased interest and understand the importance of writing.

Sometimes in schools these realistic reasons to write automatically present themselves. There will be times when the students are dissatisfied with a rule or decision that has been made within the school. During such a situation, the students could expand upon their persuasive writing skills to attempt to change the rule with which they disagree.

In other cases, students may keep pen pal letters with children in another state or country. This type of correspondence, even if accomplished via email, develops letter-writing skills in a more realistic setting than asking the students to write a fictitious letter for the teacher.

Similarly, students could write and add their own books to the library or even write books to share with younger students. Writing contests would provide another more realistic reason for students to write.

In the end, it is not the type of writing to be completed or the reason for which it is completed that is important. It is the understanding that children take away from the process that writing has a purpose in society, that writing is a relevant skill that needs to be developed.

Using these authentic methods, children will begin to see the relevance in their own lives. They will then be able to come up with their own ideas and reasons to write. This takes the skill to the next level, that of application. Bringing students to the application level is the goal of education.

Strategies for Promoting Oral Language Development and Language Comprehension

Read Alouds
(This is the cornerstone of the *Balanced Literacy Approach* for teaching reading. Therefore, it is advised that the teacher candidate and new teacher read this material carefully. This may well appear as an essay topic in the Constructed Response section of the test.)—Within the context of the *Balanced Literacy Approach* and the *Literacy Block,* the *Read-Aloud* is part of *Whole Class Activities. The book should be selected from the classroom library and be appropriate for a read-aloud.* Before reading the book to the class, the teacher needs to be familiar with it. The teacher should also *plan* or at least *know* what nuances of content, style, rhythm, and vocabulary will be emphasized in the reading.

In addition, specifically for the younger grades, the teacher should select a text that also enhances the development of phonemic awareness. This might include a text that can be used to teach rhyming, alliteration, or poetry.

Sometimes, read-aloud texts are selected for their tie-ins with the science, social studies, and mathematics curriculum.

Teachers generally aim to teach one strategy during the read-aloud, which the children will practice in small groups or independently. Among these strategies for the first grader could be print strategies and talking about books.

As the teacher reads aloud, the teacher's voice quality should highlight his/her enjoyment of the book and involvement with its text. Often in a balanced literacy classroom, the teacher reads from a specially decorated *Reader's Chair,* as do the guest readers. This chair's decorativeness, complete with comfortable throwback pillows or rocking chair style frame, is meant to set an atmosphere that will promote the children's engagement in and love for lifelong reading.

The Balanced Literacy Approach also advocates that teachers select books which children will enjoy reading aloud. Particularly accessible texts for the elementary school classroom read-alouds are collections of poetry.

Teachers must allow time for discussion during and after each Read-Aloud period. After the children have made comments, the teacher should also talk about the reading.

Use of Oral Language Activities to Promote Comprehension

Retelling

Retelling needs to be very clearly defined so that the child reader does not think that the teacher wants him or her to repeat verbatim the WHOLE story back in the retelling. A child should be able to talk comfortably and fluently about the story he/she has just read. He/she should be able to tell the main things that have happened in the story.

When a child retells a story to a teacher, the teacher needs ways to help in assessing the child's understanding. Ironically, the teacher can use some of the same strategies he/she suggests to the child to assess the child's understanding of a book with which the teacher is not familiar. These strategies include: back cover reading, scanning the table of contents, looking at the pictures, and reading the book jacket.

If the child can explain how the story turned out and provide examples to support these explanations, the teacher should try not to interrupt the child with too many questions. Children can use the text of the book to reinforce what they are saying and they can even read from it if they wish. It is also important to note that some children need to reread the text twice with the second reading being for enjoyment.

When the teacher plans to use the retelling as a way of assessing the child, then the following ground rules have to be set and made clear to the child. The teacher explains the purpose of the retelling to determine how well the child is reading at the outset of the conference.

The teacher maintains in the child's assessment notebook or in his/her assessment record what the child is saying in phrases, not sentences. Just enough is recorded to indicate whether the child actually understood the story. The teacher also tries to analyze from the retelling why the child cannot comprehend a given text. If the child's accuracy rate with the text is below 95 per cent, then the problem is at the word level, but if the accuracy rate for the text is above 95 per cent, the difficulty lies at the text level.

Development of the Reading Comprehension Skills and Strategies of Individual Students

ELL Learners bring to their classrooms different prior-knowledge concerns than do their native English language speaking peers. Some ELL students have extensive prior knowledge in their native language and can read well on or above their chronological age level in their native language. Other ELL learners come to the United States from cultures where reading was not emphasized or from circumstances where their families did not have native language literacy opportunities. Rigg and Allen (1999) offer the following four principles regarding the literacy development and prior knowledge of ELL/second-language learners:

1. In learning a language, you learn to do the things you want to do with people who are speaking that language.
2. A second language, like the first, does not develop linearly, but rather globally.
3. Language can develop in rich context.
4. Literacy develops parallel to language. So, as speaking and listening for the second language develop, so do writing and reading.

As far as retelling, it needs to be noted that English language learners have the problem of not bringing rich oral English vocabulary to the stories they are decoding. Therefore, often they "sound the stories out" well, but cannot explain what they are about, because they do not know what the words mean.

Use of Oral Reading Fluency in Facilitating Comprehension

At some point it is crucial that just as the nervous, novice bike rider finally relaxes and speeds happily off, so too must the early reader integrate graphophonic cues with semantic and structural ones. Before this is done, the oral quality of early reader's has a stilted beat to it, which of course does not promote reading engagement and enjoyment.

The teacher needs to use all of his/her drama skills to effectively model the beauty of the voice and other nuances of the text that the class is following. Children love nothing more than to mimic their teacher. If the teacher takes time each day to recite a poem with the students, the students will begin to mimic the teacher legitimately and unhesitatingly. The poem might be posted on chart paper and be up on the wall for a week.

First the teacher can model the fluent and expressive reading of this poem. Then with a pointer, the class can recite it with the teacher. As the week progresses, the class can recite it on their own.

0004 Understand the development of phonological awareness, including phonemic awareness.

Phonemic awareness and phonics are *not* the same thing – they are not interchangeable.

phonemic awareness: the understanding that the sounds in spoken language work together to make words.

phonics: the understanding that the letters represent sounds in written language.

phonological awareness: is larger. Phonological awareness includes working with words, syllables and onsets and rimes, and phonemes. It also includes recognizing rhyming, alliteration and intonation. Phonemic awareness is an important skill to teach because it improves student's word reading and reading comprehension, and it helps students learn to spell.

Activities that show children's levels of phonological awareness might include:

- rhyming activities
- clapping out syllables in words
- identifying and manipulating onsets and rimes. For example, "the first part of tap is *t-*" "the last part of pig is *–ig*"
- identifying and manipulating individual phonemes in words. For example, "The first sound in pet is /p/."

One strategy that can be used for phonemic awareness:

Blending Letter Sounds[G3]

Prompts for Graphophonic Cues

> You said ___(the child's incorrect attempt)___. Does that match the letters you see?
>
> If it were the word you just said, ___(the child's incorrect attempt)___, what would it have to start with?
>
> If it were the word you just said ___(the child's incorrect attempt)___, what would it have to end with?
>
> Look at the first letter/s . . . look at the middle letter/s . . . look at the last letter. What could it be?
>
> If you were writing ___(the child's incorrect attempt)___ what letter would you write first? What letters would go in the middle? What letters would go last?

A good strategy to use in working with individual children is to have them explain how they finally correctly identified a word that was troubling them. If prompted and habituated through one-on-one teacher/tutoring conversations, they can be quite clear about what they did to "get" the word.

If the children are already writing their own stories, the teacher might say to them: "You know when you write your own stories, you would never write any story which did not make sense. You wouldn't, and probably this writer didn't either. If you read something that does make sense, but doesn't match the letters, then it's probably not what the author wrote. This is the author's story, not your story right now, so go back to the word and see if you can find out the author's story. Later on, you might write your own story."

Use of Syllabification as a Word Identification Strategy.

Strategy: Clap Hands, Count those Syllables as They Come!! (Taberski, 2000)

The objective of this activity is for children to understand that every syllable in a polysyllabic word can be studied for its spelling patterns in the same way that monosyllabic words are studied for their spelling patterns.

The easiest way for the K–3 teacher to introduce this activity to the children is to share a familiar poem from the poetry chart (or to write out a familiar poem on a large experiential chart).

First the teacher reads the poem with the children. As they are reading it aloud, the children clap the beats of the poem and the teacher uses a colored marker to place a tic (/) above each syllable.

Next, the teacher takes letter cards and selects one of the polysyllabic words from the poem which the children have already "clapped" out.

The children use letter cards to spell that word on the sentence strip holder or it can be placed on a felt board or up against a window on display. Together, the children and teacher divide the letters into syllables and place blank letter cards between the syllables. The children identify spelling patterns they know.

Finally, and as part of continued small-group syllabification study, the children identify other polysyllabic words they clapped out from the poem. They make up the letter combinations of these words. Then they separate them into syllables with blank letter cards between the syllables.

Children who require special support in syllabification can be encouraged to use many letter cards to create a large butcher paper syllabic (in letter cards with spaces) representation of the poem or at least a few lines of the poem. They can be told that this is for use as a teaching tool for others. In this way, they authenticate their study of syllabification with a real product that can actually be referenced by peers.

DOMAIN III. READING DEVELOPMENT

0005 **Understand how to promote students' understanding of concepts of print and basic phonetic principles.**

Mature readers identify words with remarkable speed and accuracy. Fluent, automatic word recognition is a prerequisite for comprehending text. If a reader must slowly analyze many of the words in a text, memory and attention needed for comprehension are drained by word analysis.

To decode means to change communication signals into messages. Reading comprehension requires that the reader learn the code within which a message is written and be able to decode it to get the message.

There are several strategies teachers can use to promote reading fluency:

student-adult reading: A student reads one-o-one with an adult. The teacher reads first in order to model fluent reading. Next, the student reads the same passage to the adult reflecting the fluency modeled by the teacher. The student should re-read the text 3-4 times.

choral reading: Students read aloud as a group with the teacher. This is also called shared reading. Students need to be able to see the text that is being read from.

tape-assisted reading: These are also known as books on tape or CD. The student should follow along with the tape, pointing to each word in their copy of the book as the narrator reads the story aloud.

partner reading: Students pair up and take turns reading aloud to each other. Students can read the whole book to their partner, and then their partner can read the book to them. Another way to partner read is for partners to take turns reading one page at a time. The way the students are paired can be flexible too. Less fluent students can be paired with more fluent students. Also, equally fluent readers can be paired together.

reader's theatre: Students rehearse and perform before an audience of a text that includes a lot of dialogue.
Although effective reading comprehension requires identifying words automatically [fluency] (Adams, 1990, Perfetti, 1985), children do not have to be able to identify every single word or know the exact meaning of every word in a text to understand it. Indeed, Nagy (1988) says that, children can read a work with a high level of comprehension even if they do not fully know as many as 15 percent of the words within a given text.

Children develop the ability to decode and recognize words automatically. They then can extend their ability to decode to multi-syllabic words.

J. David Cooper (2004) and other advocates of the Balanced Literacy Approach feel that children become literate, effective communicators, able to comprehend by learning phonics and other aspects of word identification through the use of engaging reading texts. Engaging texts, as defined by the balanced literacy group, are those texts which contain highly predictable elements of rhyme, sound patterns, and plot. Researchers, such as Chall (1983) and Flesch (1981), support a phonics-centered foundation before the use of engaging reading texts. This is at the crux of the phonics versus whole language/ balanced literacy/ integrated language arts controversy of teaching reading.

It is important for the new teacher to be informed about both sides of this controversy, as well as the work of theorists who attempt to reconcile these two perspectives, such as Kenneth Goodman (1994). There are powerful arguments on both sides of this controversy, and each approach works wonderfully with some students and does not succeed with others.

As far as the examinations go, all that is asked of the teacher is the ability to demonstrate a familiarity with these varied perspectives. If asked on a constructed response question, teachers need to be able to show an ability to talk about teaching some aspect of reading using strategies from one or the other or a combination of both approaches.

0006　　Understand explicit, systematic phonics instruction.

systematic instruction: the instructional plan has a carefully selected set of letter-sound relationships that are organized into a logical scope and sequence.

explicit instruction: any phonics program that gives teachers precise directions for teaching.

There are different methods of explicit, systematic phonics instruction:

synthetic phonics: children learn how to make letters and combinations of letters into sounds. Students then blend the sounds together to make comprehensible words.

analytic phonics: Students do not pronounce sounds in isolation – they analyze letter-sound relationships that they have learned beforehand.

analogy-based phonics: Students use word families to identify unfamiliar words.

phonics through spelling: Students break words into phonemes and make words by writing letters for phonemes.

Systematic phonics instruction should begin in kindergarten or first grade in order to make the greatest impact on student reading. Systematic and explicit phonics gives students practice with letter-sound relationships in a certain sequence.

Non-systematic instruction often does not give enough attention to knowing vowel letter-sound relationships. The reading material that goes along with these programs is selected on such criteria as interest to children or some other literary value.

Myths about phonics instruction

There are many myths about phonics instruction. Many people believe that phonics instruction will conflict with comprehension. This is not true. On the contrary, systematic phonics instruction helps children identify and be able to decode words while reading. Reading words accurately and quickly allows children to understand text.

Some people also believe that phonics instruction will slow down the progress of some children. Again, this is a myth. Phonics instruction helps most students and contributes to their reading growth. This is another reason that flexible groups are the best way to teach early reading skills.

0007   Understand word-analysis skills and vocabulary development.

Development of Word-Analysis Skills and Strategies, Including Structural Analysis

The explicit teaching of **word analysis** requires that the teacher pre-select words from a given text for vocabulary learning. These words should be chosen based on the storyline and main ideas of the text. The educator may even want to create a story map for a narrative text or develop a graphic organizer for an expository text. Once the story mapping and/or graphic organizing have been done, the educator can compile a list of words that relate to the storyline and/or main ideas.

The number of words that require explicit teaching should only be two or three. If the number is higher than that, the children need guided reading and the text needs to be broken down into smaller sections for teaching. When broken down into smaller sections, each text section should only have two to three words which need explicit teaching.

Some researchers, including Tierney and Cunningham, believe that a few words should be taught as a means of improving comprehension.

It is up to the educator whether the vocabulary selected for teaching needs review before reading, during reading, or after reading.

Introduce vocabulary BEFORE READING if. . .

- Children are having difficulty constructing meaning on their own. Children themselves have previewed the text and indicated words they want to know.
- The teacher has seen that there are words within the text which are definitely keys necessary for reading comprehension
- The text itself, in the judgment of the teacher, contains difficult concepts for the children to grasp.

Introduce vocabulary DURING READING if . . .

- Children are already doing guided reading.
- The text has words which are crucial to its comprehension and the children will have trouble comprehending it, if they are not helped with the text.

Introduce vocabulary AFTER READING if. . .

- The children themselves have shared words which they found difficult or interesting
- The children need to expand their vocabulary
- The text itself is one that is particularly suited for vocabulary building.

Strategies to support word analysis and enhance reading comprehension include:

- Use of a graphic organizer such as a word map
- Semantic mapping
- Semantic feature analysis
- Hierarchical and linear arrays
- Preview in context
- Contextual redefinition
- Vocabulary self-collection

Structural analysis is a process of examining the words in the text for meaningful word units (affixes, base words, and inflected endings). There are six word types that are formed and therefore can be analyzed using structural analysis strategies. They include:

1. Common prefixes or suffixes added to a known word ending with a consonant
2. Adding the suffix *–ed* to words that end with consonants
3. Compound words
4. Adding endings to words that end with the letter *e*
5. Adding endings to words that end with the letter *y*
6. Adding affixes to multisyllabic words

When[G4] teaching and using structural analysis procedures in the primary grades, teachers should remember to make sound decisions on which to introduce and teach. Keeping in mind the number of primary words in which each affix appears and how similar they are will help the teacher make the instructional process smoother and more valuable to the students.

Adding affixes to words can be started when students are able to read a list of one-syllable words by sight at a rate of approximately 20 words correct per minute. At the primary level, there is a recommended sequence for introducing affixes. The steps in this process are:

- Start by introducing the affix in the letter-sound correspondence format
- Practice the affix in isolation for a few days.
- Provide words for practice which contain the affix (word lists/flash card).
- Move from word lists to passage reading, which includes words with the affix (and some from the word lists/flash cards).

Structural Analysis Activities

Word Study Group
This involves the teacher taking time to meet with children from grades 3–6 in a small group of no more than six children for a word study session. Taberski (2000) suggests that this meeting take place next to the word wall. The children selected for this group are those who need to focus more on the relationship between spelling patterns and consonant sounds.

It is important that this not be a formalized traditional reading group that meets at a set time each week or biweekly. Rather the group should be spontaneously formed by the teacher based on the teacher's quick inventory of the selected children's needs at the start of the week. Taberski has templates in her book of *Guided Reading Planning Sheets.* These sheets are essentially targeted word and other skills sheets with her written dated observations of children who are in need of support to develop a given skill.

The teacher should try to meet with this group for at least two consecutive 20-minute periods daily. Over those two meetings, the teacher can model a *Making Words Activity.* Once the teacher has modeled making words the first day, the children would then make their own words. On the second day, the children would "sort" their words.

Other topics for a word study group within the framework of the *Balanced Literacy Approach* that Taberski advocates are: inflectional endings, prefixes and suffixes, and/or common spelling patterns. These are covered later in this chapter.

It should be noted that this activity would be classified by theorists as a structural analysis activity because the structural components (i.e. prefixes, suffixes, and spelling patterns) of the words are being studied.

Discussion Circles

J. David Cooper (2004) believes that children should not be "taught" vocabulary and structural analysis skills. Flesch and E. D. Hirsch, key theorists of the phonics approach and advocates of Cultural Literacy (a term coined and associated with E. D. Hirsch), believe that specific vocabulary words at various grade and age levels need to be mastered and must be explicitly taught in schools. As far as Cooper is concerned, all the necessary and meaningful vocabulary (for the child and ultimately adult reader) can't possibly be taught in schools. To Cooper it is far more important that the children be made aware of and become interested in learning words by themselves. Cooper feels that through the child's reading and writing, he/she develops a love for and a sense of "ownership" of words. All of Cooper's suggested structural analysis word strategies are therefore designed to foster the child's love of words and a desire to "own" more of them through reading and writing.

Discussion Circles is an activity that fits nicely into the balanced literacy lesson format. After the children conclude a particular text, Cooper suggests they respond to the book in discussion circles. Among the prompts, the teacher-coach might suggest that the children focus on words of interest they encountered in the text. These can also be words that they heard if the text was read aloud. Children can be asked to share something funny or upsetting or unusual about the words they have read. Through this focus on children's response to words as the center of the discussion circle, peers become more interested in word study.

Banking, Booking, and Filing It: Making Words Their Own
Children can realize the goal of making words their own and exploring word structures through creating concrete objects or displays that demonstrate the words they own.

Encourage children to create and maintain their own files of words they have learned or are interested in learning. Although they can categorize these files according to their own interests, they should develop files using science, history, physical education, fine arts, dance, and technology content. Newspapers and web resources approved by the teacher are excellent sources for such words. In addition to benefiting the students, this filing activity provides the teacher with the opportunity to instruct children in age-appropriate and grade-level research skills. Even children in grades 2 and 3 can begin simplified bibliographies and webliographies for their "found" words. They can learn how to annotate and note the page of a newspaper, book, or URL for a particular word.

Children can also copy down words as they appear in the text (print or electronic). If appropriate, they can place the words found for given topics or content in an actual bank of their own making or print the words on cards. This allows for differentiated word study and appeals to those children who are kinesthetic and spatial learners. Of course, children can also choose to create their own word books showcasing their specialized vocabulary and descriptions of how they identified or hunted down their words. Richard Scarry, watch out! Scarry books can be anchor books to inspire this structural analysis activity. ELL learners can share their accounts in their native language first and then translate (with the help of the teacher) these accounts into English, posting both the native language and the English language versions for peers to view.

Write Out Your Words, Write with Your Words. Ownership of words can be demonstrated by having the children use the words in their writings. The children can author a procedural narrative (a step-by-step description) of how they went about their word searches to compile the words they found for any of the activities. If the children are in grades K–1, or if the children are struggling readers and writers, their procedural narratives can be dictated. Then they can be posted by the teacher.

ELL students can share their accounts in their native language first and then translate (with the help of the teacher) these accounts into English with both the native language and the English language versions of the word exploration posted.

Children with special needs may model a word box on a specific holiday theme, genre, or science/social studies topic with the teacher. Initially this can be done as a whole class. As the children become more confident, they can work with peers or with a paraprofessional to create their own individual or small team/pair word boxes.

Special needs children can create a storyboard with the support of a paraprofessional, their teacher, or a resource specialist. They can also narrate their story of how they all found the words, using a tape recorder.

Word Study Museum in the Classroom

This strategy has been presented in detail so it can be used by the teachers within their own classrooms. In addition, the way the activity is described and the mention at the end of the description of how the activity can address family literacy, ELL, and special needs children's talents, provides an example of other audiences a teacher should consider in curriculum design.

Almost every general education teacher and reading specialist will have to differentiate instruction to address the needs of special education and ELL learners. Family or shared literacy is a major component of all literacy instruction. Children can create a single or multiple exhibits, museum style, within their classrooms celebrating their word study. They can build actual representations of the type of study they have done including word trees (made out of cardboard or foam board), elaborate word boxes and games, word history timelines or murals, and word study maps. They can develop online animations, *Kidspiration* graphic organizers, *QuickTime* movies, digital photo essays, and PowerPoint presentations to share the words they have identified.

The classroom, gym, or cafeteria can be transformed into a gallery space. Children can author brochure descriptions for their individual, team, or class exhibits. Some children can volunteer to be tour guides or docents for the experience. Other children can work to create a banner for the *Word Study Museum*. The children can name the museum themselves and send out invitations to its opening. Invitations can be sent to parents, community, staff members, peers, and younger classes.

Depending on their age and grade level, children can also develop interactive games and quizzes focused on particular exhibits. An artist or a team of class artists can design a poster for the exhibit, while other children choose to build the exhibits. Another small group can work on signage and a catalogue or register of objects within the exhibit. Greeters who will welcome parents and peers to the exhibit can be trained and can develop their own scripts.

If the children are in grades 4–6, they can also develop their own visitor feedback forms and design word-themed souvenirs. The whole museum can be photographed, with the pictures hung later near the word walls along with a description of the event. Of course, the children can use many of their newly recognized and owned words to describe the event.

The *Word Study Museum* activity can be used with either a phonics-based or a Balanced Literacy Approach. It promotes additional writing, researching, discussing, and reading about words.

It is also an excellent family literacy strategy in that families can develop their own word exhibits at home. This activity can also support and celebrate learners with disabilities. It can be presented in dual languages by children who are ELL learners and fluent in more than a single language.

This aspect of vocabulary development is to help children look for structural elements within words which they can use independently to help them determine meaning.

Some teachers choose to directly teach structural analysis, in particular, those who teach by following the phonics-centered approach for reading. Other teachers, who follow the balanced literacy approach, introduce the structural components as part of mini lessons that are focused on the students' reading and writing.

Structural analysis of words as defined by J. David Cooper (2004) involves the study of significant word parts. This analysis can help the child with pronunciation and constructing meaning.

Definition questions—multiple choice questions which have only a single right answer—test whether the teacher candidate has memorized the appropriate terminology. They constitute no less than 15% of the multiple choice questions on the test. Therefore, by taking the time to memorize these easy definitions, scores are likely to improve. Structural analysis components are explicitly taught in schools which advocate the phonics-centered approach and are also incorporated into the word work component of the schools which advocate the balanced literacy approach for instruction. The list of terms below is generally recognized as the key structural analysis components.

Knowledge of Greek and Latin Roots That Form English Words

Knowledge of Greek and Latin roots which comprise English words can measurably enhance children's reading skills and can also enrich their writing.

Word Webs

Taberski (2000) does not advocate teaching Greek and Latin derivatives in the abstract to young children. However, when she comes across (as is common and natural) specific Greek and Latin roots while reading to children, she uses that opportunity to introduce children to these rich resources.

For example, during readings on rodents (a favorite of first and second graders), Taberski draws her class's attention to the fact that beavers gnaw at things with their teeth. She then connects the root *dent* with other words with which the children are familiar. The children then volunteer *dentist, dental, denture.* Taberski begins to place these in a graphic organizer, or word web.

When she has tapped the extent of the children's prior knowledge of *dent* words, she shares with them the fact that *dens/dentis* is the Latin word for teeth. Then she introduces the word *indent,* which she has already previewed with them as part of their conventions of print study. She helps them to see that the *indenting* of the first line of a paragraph can even be related to the *teeth* Latin root in that it looks like a "print" bite was taken out of the paragraph.

Taberski displays the word web in the Word Wall Chart section of her room. The class is encouraged throughout, say, a week's time to look for other words to add to the web. Taberski stresses that for her, as an elementary teacher of reading and writing, the key element of the Greek and Latin word root web activity is the children's coming to understand that if they know what a Greek or Latin word root means, they can use that knowledge to figure out what other words mean.

She feels the key concept is to model and demonstrate for children how fun and fascinating Greek and Latin root study can be.

Greek and Latin Roots Word Webs with an Assist from the Internet
Older children in grades 3–6 can build on this initial activity by searching online for additional words with a particular Greek or Latin root which has been introduced in class.

They can easily do this in a way that authentically ties in with their own interests and experiences by reading reviews for a book which has been a read-aloud online or by just reading the summaries of the day's news and printing out those words which appear in the stories online that share the root discussed.

The children can be encouraged to circle these instances of their Latin or Greek root and also to document the exact date and URL for the citation. These can be posted as part of their own online web in the word wall section study area. If the school or class has a website or webpage, the children can post this data there as a special Greek and Latin root- word page.

Expanding the concept of the Greek and Latin word web from the printed page to the Internet nicely inculcates the child in the habits of lifelong reading combined with online researching. This beginning expository research will serve them well in intermediate level content area work and beyond.

Techniques for Identifying Compound Words
The teaching of compound words should utilize structural analysis techniques. (See section on structural analysis). Here are some other strategies for helping students to identify and read compound words.

- Use songs and actions to help children understand the concept that compound words are two smaller words joined together to make one bigger word
- Use games like *Concentration, Memory,* and *Go Fish* for students to practice reading compound words
- Use word sorts to have students distinguish between compound words and non-examples of compound words

Identification of Homographs
Homographs are words that are spelled the same but have different meanings. A subgroup within this area includes words that are spelled the same, have different meanings, and are pronounced differently. Some examples of homographs include:

- Lie
- Tear
- Bow
- Fair
- Bass

Teaching homographs can be interesting and fun for the students, incorporating them into passages where the students can use the context clues to decipher the different meanings of the homographs. Using games is also a good strategy to help students understand multiple meaning words. Jokes and riddles are usually based on homographs, and students love to make collections or books of these.

Semantic Feature Analysis
This technique for enhancing vocabulary skills by using semantic cues is based on the research of Johnson and Pearson (1984) and Anders and Bos (1986). It involves young children in setting up a feature analysis grid of various subject content words which is an outgrowth of their discussion about these words.

For instance, Cooper (2004) includes a sample of a Semantic Features Analysis Grid for Vegetables.

Vegetables	Green	Have Peels	Eat Raw	Seeds
Carrots	–	+	+	–
Cabbage	+	–	+	–

Note: that the use of the + for yes, – for no, and possible use for + and – if a vegetable like squash could be both green and yellow.

Teachers of children in grade one and beyond can design their own semantic analysis grids to meet their students' needs and to align with the topics the children are learning. Select a category or class of words, e.g., planets, rodent family members, winter words, or weather words.

Use the left side of the grid to list at least three if not more items that fit this category. The number of actual items listed will depend on the age and grade level of the children with three or four items fine for K–1 and up to 10–15 for grades 5 and 6. Brainstorm with the children. If better suited to the class, the teacher may list his/her own features that the items have in common. From the example excerpted from *Cooper's Literacy: Helping Children Construct Meaning* (2004), common features that are usually easy to identify include vegetables' green color, peels, and seeds.

Show the children how to insert the notations +, –, and even ? (if they are not certain) on the grid. The teacher might also explore with the children the possibility that an item could get both a + and a –. For example, a vegetable like broccoli might be eaten cooked or raw depending on taste and squash can be green or yellow.

Whatever the length of the grid when first presented to the children (perhaps as a semantic cue lesson in and of itself tied in to a text being read in class), make certain that the grid as presented and filled out is not the end of the activity.

Children can use it as a model for developing their own semantic features grids and share them with the whole class. Child-developed grids can become part of a Word Work center in the classroom or even be published in a Word Study Games book by the class as a whole. Such a publication can be shared with parents during open school week and evening visits and with peer classes.

Key Structural Analysis Components Definitions

Root Word
This is a word from which another word is developed. The second word can be said to have its "root" in the first, such as *vis, to see,* in visor or vision. This structural component can be illustrated by a tree with roots to display the meaning for children. Children may also want to literally construct root words using cardboard trees to create word family models.

ELL students can construct these models for their native language root-word families, as well for the English language words they are learning. ELL students in the 5th and 6th grade may even appreciate analyzing the different root structures for contrasts and similarities between their native language and English. Learners with special needs can focus in small groups or individually with a paraprofessional on building root-word models.

Base Words

These are stand-alone linguistic units which cannot be deconstructed or broken down into smaller words. For example, in the word *retell*, the base word is "tell."

Contractions

These are shortened forms of two words in which a letter or letters have been deleted. These deleted letters have been replaced by an apostrophe.

Prefixes

These are beginning units of meaning which can be added (the vocabulary word for this type of structural adding is "affixed") to a base word or root word. They cannot stand alone. They are also sometimes known as "bound morphemes" meaning that they cannot stand alone as a base word. Examples are *re-, un-,* and *mis-*.

Suffixes

These are ending units of meaning which can be "affixed" or added on to the ends of root or base words. Suffixes transform the original meanings of base and root words. Like prefixes, they are also known as "bound morphemes," because they cannot stand alone as words. Examples are *-less, -ful*, and *-tion*.

Compound Words

These occur when two or more base words are connected to form a new word. The meaning of the new word is in some way connected with that of the base word. Examples are *firefighter, newspaper*, and *pigtail*.

Inflectional Endings

These are types of suffixes that impart a new meaning to the base or root word. These endings in particular change the gender, number, tense, or form of the base or root words. Just like other suffixes, these are also termed "bound morphemes." Examples are *–s* or *-ed*.

Familiarity with word **roots** (the basic elements of words) and with **prefixes** can help one determine the meanings of unknown words. Following is a partial list of roots and prefixes. It might be useful to review these.

Root	Meaning	Example
aqua	water	aqualung
astro	stars	astrology
bio	life	biology
carn	meat	carnivorous
circum	around	circumnavigate
geo	earth	geology
herb	plant	herbivorous
mal	bad	malicious
neo	new	neonatal
tele	distant	telescope
un-	not	unnamed
re-	again	reenter
il-	not	illegible
pre-	before	preset
mis-	incorrectly	misstate
in-	not	informal
anti-	against	antiwar
de-	opposite	derail
post-	after	postwar
ir-	not	irresponsible

Word Forms

Sometimes a very familiar word can appear as a different part of speech. For example, you may have heard that *fraud* involves a criminal misrepresentation, so when it appears as the adjective form *fraudulent*, (e.g., "He was suspected of *fraudulent* activities.") you can make an educated guess. You probably know that something out-of-date is *obsolete;* therefore, when you read about "built-in *obsolescence,*" you can detect the meaning of the unfamiliar word.

It is inevitable in reading that students will come across words they are unable to read. When this happens, the student will need a variety of strategies to draw upon to figure out the unknown word and gather meaning from the word and text.

When they encounter unknown words, students typically begin with decoding or the application of phonics skills. If they are unable to correctly decode the word, they may use other strategies such as structural analysis and context clues.

In structural analysis, students use word patterns and parts they recognize to figure out unknown words. When decoding, students tend to look at no more than two letters together. In contrast, structural analysis allows students to look at larger portions of words.

Contextual reading is something we all do from a very young age to adult years. Sometimes, regardless of our ability to decode or apply structural analysis, we are unable to read certain words. In this case, readers can use other words in the sentence or paragraph to help decide the unknown word.

Good readers use the syntax, the manner in which the sentence is put together, to help determine meaning from context. They also find ways to put the sentence or passage in their own words or look for contrasting ideas. All of these strategies help the reader to draw meaning from what is being read. This frame of reference helps to provide more details for the reader. Contrast is also a method readers may use to build context or determine meaning.

All of these strategies together help readers develop their comprehension ability. However, some words have more than one meaning. In this case, the student may be able to identify the word but have difficulty determining meaning. In some cases, meaning can be confusing as the student only knows one meaning of the word, and when reading, it simply does not make sense.

It is in this instance that the use of context clues can be most beneficial. Students can begin to learn more than one meaning by basing their analysis on the rest of the words in the passage. In this way, they can learn the multiple meanings of words without having to rely on skill and drill vocabulary activities.

Context clues help readers determine the meanings of unfamiliar words. The context of a word is the sentence or sentences that surround the word.

Sentence Clues

Often, a writer will actually **define** a difficult or particularly important word for you the first time it appears in a passage. Phrases such as *that is, such as, which is,* or *is called* might announce the writer's intention to give just the definition you need. Occasionally, a writer will simply use a synonym (a word that means the same thing) or a near-synonym joined by the word *or*. Look at the following examples:

> The <u>credibility</u>, *that is to say the believability, of the witness was called into question by evidence of previous perjury.*

Read the following sentences, and attempt to determine the meanings of the words in bold print.

> The **luminosity** *of the room was so incredible that there was no need for lights.*

If there were no need for lights, then one must assume that the word luminosity has something to do with giving off light. The definition of luminosity is *the emission of light.*

> *Jamie could not understand Joe's feelings. His mood swings made understanding him somewhat of an* **enigma.**

The fact that he could not be understood made him somewhat of a puzzle. The definition of enigma is *a mystery or puzzle.*

When students are reading something that does not make sense, they should start with using the strategies described in detail in Skill 6.2 (context clues, syntax, decoding, and semantics). However, there are other times when it is necessary to be more specific in determining if the definition is correctly inferred. In these cases, the reader may need to look outside of the text at additional resources to ensure their accuracy. Students might begin with the glossary, if included, as it is located within the same text. However, other times, they may need to refer to some other mode of finding the meaning or pronunciation of the words. Students may use a dictionary to help with these skills.

Dictionary skills are important for students to learn and use regularly. The dictionary can provide the reader with several different meanings for the word. The student can use the different meanings provided along with the contextual information they gained from the text to determine which meaning is most appropriate. They can also use the pronunciation guide to determine how to say the word, which will help later in reading.

Sometimes, it is helpful to use synonyms or antonyms to help clarify meaning. A thesaurus is formatted similar to a dictionary in design and layout; however, instead of providing the definition and pronunciation of the words, it provides words that are synonyms and antonyms for the word given. This can help the student to put the passage in more reader friendly terms or in terms with which they are more familiar. The use of synonyms and antonyms is an excellent way to build vocabulary.

In today's society, all of these tools can be found in various technological forms. There are online dictionaries and thesauruses. Additionally, there are pocket personal electronic dictionaries with built-in thesauruses. There is also a reading pen, which teachers use to help determine unknown words. The tip of the pen is rubbed lightly across the unknown word. The computer-generated voice built into the pen speaks it orally with the correct pronunciation for the student to hear. Then it provides the definition, synonyms, and antonyms on a digital display. On some models, this information can also be repeated orally.

Punctuation at the sentence level is often a clue to the meaning of a word. Commas, parentheses, quotation marks, and dashes tell the reader that the writer is offering a definition.

> *A tendency toward <u>hyperbole</u>, extravagant exaggeration, is a common flaw among persuasive writers.*

> *Political <u>apathy</u>—lack of interest—can lead to the death of the state.*

A writer might simply give an **explanation** in other words that you can understand in the same sentence.

> *The <u>xenophobic</u> townspeople were suspicious of every foreigner.*

Writers also explain a word in terms of its **opposite** at the sentence level.

> *His <u>incarceration</u> was ended, and he was elated to be out of jail.*
> *Nothing would <u>assuage</u> or lessen the child's grief.*

Practice Questions: Read the following sentences and attempt to determine the meanings of the underlined words.

1. Farmer John got a two-horse plow and went to work. Straight <u>furrows</u> stretched out behind him.

   The word <u>furrows</u> means

   (A) long cuts made by a plow
   (B) vast, open fields
   (C) rows of corn
   (D) pairs of hitched horses

2. The survivors struggled ahead, <u>shambling</u> through the terrible cold, doing their best not to fall.

   The word <u>shambling</u> means

   (A) frozen in place
   (B) running
   (C) shivering uncontrollably
   (D) walking awkwardly

The context for a word goes beyond the sentence in which it appears. At times, the writer uses adjacent (adjoining) sentences to present an explanation or definition.

> *The two dollars for the car repair would have to come out of the <u>contingency</u> fund. Fortunately, Angela's father had taught her to keep some money set aside for just such emergencies.*

Analysis: The second sentence offers a clue to the definition of *contingency* as used in this sentence—*emergencies*. Therefore, a fund for contingencies would be money tucked away for unforeseen and/or urgent events.

Entire passage clues

On occasion, you must look at an entire paragraph or passage to figure out the definition of a word or term. In the following paragraph, notice how the word *nostalgia* undergoes a form of extended definition throughout the selection rather than in just one sentence.

> *The word <u>nostalgia</u> links Greek words for "away from home" and "pain." If you are feeling <u>nostalgic</u>, then you are probably in some physical distress or discomfort, suffering from a feeling of alienation and separation from loved ones or loved places. <u>Nostalgia</u> is that awful feeling you remember the first time you went away to camp or spent the weekend with a friend's family—homesickness, or some condition even more painful than that. However, in common use, <u>nostalgia</u> has come to have associations that are more sentimental. A few years back, for example, a <u>nostalgia</u> craze had to do with the 1950s. We resurrected poodle skirts and saddle shoes, built new restaurants to look like old ones, and tried to make chicken à la king just as mother probably never made it. In TV situation comedies, we recreated a pleasant world that probably never existed and relished our <u>nostalgia</u>, longing for a homey, comfortable lost time.*

The context for a word is the written passage that surrounds it. Sometimes the writer offers synonyms—words that have nearly the same meaning. Context clues can appear within the sentence itself, within the preceding and/or following sentence(s), or in the passage as a whole.

Extending a Reader's Understanding of Familiar Words

Dictionary Use
Dictionaries are useful for spelling, writing, and reading. It is very important to initially expose and habituate students to enjoy using the dictionary.

Cooper (2004) suggests that the following be kept in mind as the teacher of grades K–6 introduces and then habituates children to a lifelong fascination with the dictionary and vocabulary acquisition.

Requesting or suggesting that children look up a word in the dictionary should be an invitation to a wonderful exploration, not a punishment or busy work that has no reference to their current reading assignment.

Model the correct way to use the dictionary for children even as late as the third to sixth grade. Many have never been taught proper dictionary skills. The teacher needs to demonstrate to the children that as an adult reader and writer, he/she routinely and happily uses the dictionary and learns new information that makes him or her better at reading and writing.

Cooper believes in beginning dictionary study and use as early as kindergarten; this is now very possible because of the proliferation of lush picture dictionaries that can be introduced at that grade level. He also suggests that children not only look at these picture dictionaries, but also begin to make dictionaries of their own at this grade level filled with pictures and beginning words. As children join the circle of lexicographers, they will begin to see themselves as compilers and users of dictionaries. Of course, this will support their ongoing vocabulary development.

In early grade levels, use of the dictionary can nicely complement the children's mastery of the alphabet. They should be given whole-class and small-group practice in locating words.

As the children progress with their phonetic skills, the dictionary can be used to show them phonetic re-spelling using the pronunciation key.

Older children in grades 3 and beyond need explicit teacher demonstrations and practice in the use of guide words. They also need to begin to learn about the hierarchies of various word meanings. In the upper grades, children should also explore using special content dictionaries and glossaries located in the backs of their books.

0008   Understand the development of reading fluency and reading comprehension.

Decoding

In the late 1960s and early 1970s, many reading specialists, most prominently the linguist Charles C. Fries (1962), believed that successful decoding resulted in reading comprehension. This meant that if children could sound out the words, they would then automatically be able to comprehend the words. Many teachers of reading and many reading texts still subscribe to this theory.

Asking questions

Another theory or approach to the teaching of reading that gained currency in the late sixties and the early seventies was the importance of asking inferential and critical thinking questions of the reader which would challenge and engage the children in the text. This approach to reading went beyond the literal level of what was stated in the text to an inferential level of using text clues to make predictions and to a critical level of involving the child in evaluating the text. While asking engaging and thought-provoking questions is still viewed as part of the teaching of reading, it is only viewed currently as a component of the teaching of reading.

Comprehension "Skills"

As various reading theories, practices, and approaches percolated during the 1970s and 1980s, many educators and researchers in the field came to believe that the teacher of reading had to teach a set of discrete "Comprehension Skills" (Otto et al., 1977). Therefore, the reading teacher became the teacher of each individual comprehension skill. Children in such classrooms came away with: main idea, sequence, cause and effect, and other concepts that were supposed to make them better comprehenders. However, did it make them lifelong readers?

Transactional Approach

During the late 1970s and early 1980s, researchers in the field of education, psychology, and linguistics, began to examine how the reader comprehends. Among them was Louise Rosenblatt who posited that reading is a transaction between the reader and the text. It is Rosenblatt (1978) who explained successful reading as the reader constructing a meaning from the text that reflected both the reader and the text. She differentiates two separate modes in the experience of reading: *efferent* and *aesthetic*. They each have a distinct purpose. Efferent reading is looking for and remembering information to use functionally. Examples would be filling out a job application, reading a story in preparation for a test, or reading a newspaper article to find out who won the state basketball championship. Aesthetic reading is done to connect one's own life to the text, to be swept away by the beauty of a poem, or to respond emotionally to a book such as *Bridge to Terabithia*.

These differing purposes call for somewhat different reading strategies. For example, one might skim a newspaper article for basketball information but read a poem closely ten times and create mental images of different passages. Lastly, when children are asked to read all fiction differently (What's the setting? What's the main conflict in the plot? There will be a test on this on Thursday!), it can thwart a child's joy in the written word and work against the student's desire to be a lifelong reader.

Bottom-up, Top-down, Interactional Theories of Reading

Bottom-up theories of reading assume that children learn from part-to-whole starting with the smallest segments possible. Instruction begins with a strong phonics approach, learning letter–sound relationships and often using basal readers or *decodable books*. Decodable books are vocabulary controlled using language from word families with high predictability. Thus we get sentences like "Nan has a tan fan." Reading is seen as skills based, and the skills are taught one at a time.

Top-down theories of reading suggest that reading begins with the reader's knowledge, not the print. Children are seen as having a drive to construct meaning. This stance views reading as moving from the whole to the parts. An early top-down theory was the *whole word* approach. Children memorized high-frequency words to assist them in reading the *Dick and Jane* books of the 1930s.

Then teachers helped children discover letter–sound correspondences in what they read. A more recent top-down theory is the *whole language* approach. This approach was influenced by research on how young children learned language. It was thought that children could learn to read as naturally as they learned to talk. Children were surrounded by print in their classrooms, using quality literature often printed in Big Books. They were viewed as writers from the start. Advocates of whole language viewed the "skill 'em—drill 'em—kill 'em" approach based on bottom-up theories as a deadly dull introduction to the world of reading.

Interactive theories of reading combine the strengths of both bottom-up and top-down approaches. Right from students' earliest days in school, teachers must teach decoding, vocabulary, and comprehension skills that support children's drive for meaning and promote a stimulating exchange with high-quality literary texts. Strategies include shared, guided, and independent reading, Big Books, reading and writing workshops, and the like. Today this approach is called the *Balanced Literacy Approach.* It is considered to be a synthesis of the best from bottom-up and top-down methods.

Literacy and Literacy Learning

To be literate in the 21st century means more than being able to read and write. To live well and happily in today's society, one must be able to read not only newspapers and books, but e-mails, blogs, directions for cell phone use, and the like. There is a "disconnect" between the isolated reading comprehension skills the schools were teaching and the literacy skills including listening and speaking that are crucial for employment and personal and academic success. Thornburg (1992, 2003) has also noted that technology capacities and the ability to communicate online are now integral parts of our sense of literacy.

Cooper (2004) views literacy as reading, writing, thinking, listening, viewing, and discussing. These are not viewed as separate activities or components of instruction, but rather as developing and being nurtured simultaneously and interactively. Children learn these abilities by engaging in authentic explorations, readings, projects and experiences.

Just as the child learning to ride a bike goes through various approximations before learning how to actually ride, the reader uses the scaffold (support) of the teacher to go through various approximations before developing his/her own independent literacy skills and capacities..

Emergent Literacy
This concept states that young children are emerging into reading and writing with no real beginning or ending point. Children are introduced into the word of print as soon as their parents read board books to them at the age of one or two. When children scribble write or use invented spelling during their preschool years, they reveal themselves as detectives of the written word, having watched parents and teachers make lists, write thank-you notes, or leave messages. This view of the reader assumes that all children have a drive to make meaning out of print and will begin doing it almost on their own if surrounded by a print-rich environment.

Reading Readiness
In contrast to emergent literacy, this approach assumes that all children must have mastered a sequence of reading skills *before* they can begin to read.

Prior Knowledge, Schemata, Background, and Comprehension

Schemata are structures that represent generic concepts stored in our memory (Rumelhart 1980). Young children develop their schemata through experiences.

Prior knowledge and the lack of experiences in some cases influence comprehension. The more closely the reader's experiences and schemata approximate those of the writer, the more likely the reader is to comprehend the text. Schemata deficits among children from other-language backgrounds or struggling socio-economic family structures indicate the need for intense teacher support as these children become emergent and early readers.

Often the teacher will have to model and scaffold for the child the steps to form a schemata from the information provided in a text.

Comprehension

Cooper defines comprehension as "a strategic process by which readers construct or assign meaning to a text by using the clues in the text and their own prior knowledge." We view comprehension as a process where the reader transacts with the text to construct or assign meaning. Reading and writing are both interconnected and mutually supportive. Comprehension is a strategic process in which readers adjust their reading to suit their reading purpose and the type or genre of text they are reading. Narrative and expository texts require different reading approaches because of their different text structures.

Strategic readers also call into play their metacognitive capacities as they analyze texts so that they are aware of the skills needed to construct meaning from the text structure.

The Role of Literature in Developing Literacy

The Balanced Literacy Approach advocates the use of "real literature"—recognized works from the best children's fiction and non-fiction trade books and winners of such awards as the Newbery and Caldecott medals for helping children develop literacy.

Balanced literacy advocates argue that:

- Real literature engages young readers and assures that they will become lifelong readers.

- Real literature also offers readers a language base that can help them expand their expressiveness as readers and as writers.

- Real literature is easier to read and understand than grade-leveled texts

There are districts in the United States where the phonics-only approach is heavily embedded. However, the majority of school districts would describe their approach to reading as the Balanced Literacy Approach which includes phonics work as well as the use of real literature texts. To contrast the phonics and Balanced Literacy Approaches as opposite is inaccurate, since a balanced approach includes both.

It is important to go online and to visit the key resources of the National Council of Teachers of English (NCTE) and the International Reading Association (IRA) to keep abreast of the latest research in the field.

The creation of the meeting area and the reading chair (sometimes a rocking chair) with throw pillows around it promotes a love of reading. Beyond that, some classrooms have adopted an author's hat, decorated with the pictures of famous authors and book characters which children wear when they read from their own works.

Many classrooms also have children's storyboards, artwork, story maps, pop-up books, and "in the style of" writing inspired by specific authors. Some teachers buy calendars for the daily schedule which celebrate children's authors or types of literature. Children are also encouraged to bring in public library books and special books from their home libraries. The teacher can model this habit of sharing beautiful books and inviting stories from his/her home library.

In addition, news stories about children's authors, series books, television versions of books, theatrical film versions of books, stuffed toy book character decorations and other memorabilia related to books can be used to decorate the room

Various chain book stores including Barnes and Nobles and Borders give out free book marks and promotional display materials related to children's books which can be available in the room for children to use as they read independently or in their guided groups. They might even use these artistic models to inspire their own book themed artifacts.

Asking students to complete an interest survey will give the teacher clues as to what themes or topics he/she can use when looking for age- and grade-appropriate literature for the classroom. Reading conferences are another way teachers can find out what students like to read. Teachers can compile a class list of favorite books and display it in the classroom. One activity that doubles as a literacy response and an enhancement for other students is to have the students rate a book and recommend it for others to read.

Reading fluency has been shown to have strong correlations to comprehension skills, which are the goal of any reading activity. Therefore, it is very important for students to have well developed fluency skills. For students who do not naturally develop their fluency skills, the teacher must provide strategies or activities that help develop them.

Choral Reading
Choral reading is an effective reading strategy used to increase fluency. Students can read with a group or the teacher to build their fluency. In this strategy, reading should be done at an appropriate pace and with good prosody.

Reader's Theater
This strategy helps to bring drama back into the classroom by creating, scripts with different parts for different characters. The students practice the script in small groups for a few days, and then they complete a reading with good fluent reading for their peers. There is no preparation of costumes or set design, but it allows the students to have the practice of reading different parts.

Frequent Independent Reading

The more opportunity students have to practice reading, the more fluent they will become. The key is that the reading is on their independent level and the text is enjoyable for the reader. Students need to have some independent reading time daily.

Paired Reading

Students are sometimes the best teachers. Paired reading is an opportunity for them to provide effective instruction to their peers. For the struggling readers, this is an excellent strategy to increase reading fluency. Sometimes, students can graph the results of their *words correct per minute* (wcpm) with their student helpers to have a visual representation of their progress. There are different things to consider when pairing students, including: reading level, ability to work together and stay on task, and appropriate materials for both partners to read.

Repeated Readings

Repeated reading passages are one of the most effective strategies for increasing oral reading fluency. This can be done individually or in pairs. Tying graphing, paired reading, and repeated oral reading into one time frame within the classroom can provide teachers and students with a specific strategy easily incorporated for a few minutes a day into the classroom routine.

Previously, we described methods used to increase reading fluency. Most teachers would immediately equate fluency with the amount of words per minute read correctly. However, reading fluency is more than reading speed. Students must also demonstrate good prosody. Prosody covers the ideas of reading with expression, appropriate phrasing, and good inflection.

Generally considered a part of fluency, prosody is an important element on all rubrics used to evaluate reading fluency. Prosody is what takes otherwise robotic reading and makes it into something enjoyable to hear. The punctuation we use as part of grammar provides the students the cues for reading with good prosody.

Modeling is one of the most effective strategies a teacher can use with students to enhance their prosody skills. Teachers need to provide examples of good reading, as well as nonexamples where the teacher reads "robotically." In this way, students can hear the differences between good oral reading and poor oral reading.

Prosody can only be built by using oral reading, so any of the already mentioned strategies for improving fluency can also be used to increase the prosody of the same students. It is important for students to clearly understand that reading is not a race. It is not all about the number of words read correctly in a minute, but rather about the number of well-read words.

While the majority of reading will occur silently in the student's head, it is necessary to take the time to practice reading out loud to ensure students develop this more natural flow of language. It will be more likely this phrasing and expression will then transfer into the silent reading if the students are able to perform it orally. If they are unable to do the task orally, the reading in their head may be just as robotic or choppy which can impact comprehension in a negative manner.

Sequence of Events

The ability to organize events or steps provided in a passage (especially when presented in random order) serves a useful purpose, and it encourages the development of logical thinking and the processes of analysis and evaluation.

One way to identify sequence is to note transition words, such as "first" or "then." Another clue is to use enumeration to identify the proper order.

Working through and discussing examples, such as the one below, with your students helps students to gain valuable practice in sequencing events.

Practice Question: Identify the proper order of events or steps.

1. Matt had tied a knot in his shoelace.
2. Matt put on his green socks because they were clean and complemented the brown slacks he was wearing.
3. Matt took a bath and trimmed his toenails.
4. Matt put on his brown slacks.

Answer: The proper order of events is 3, 4, 2, and 1.

Cause and Effect

A cause is the necessary source of a particular outcome. If a writer were addressing the questions, "How will the new tax laws affect small businesses?" or "Why has there been such political unrest in Somalia?" he or she would use cause and effect as an organizational pattern to structure his or her response. In the first case, the writer would emphasize effects of the tax legislation as they apply to owners of small businesses. In the second, he/she would focus on causes for the current political situation in Somalia.

Some word clues that identify a cause-effect passage are *accordingly, as a result, therefore, because, consequently, hence, in short, thus, then, due to* and *so on.*

Sample passage:

> *Simply put, inflation is an increase in price levels. It happens when a government prints more currency than is already in circulation, and there is, consequently, additional money available for the same amount of goods or services. There might be multiple reasons for a government to crank up the printing presses. A war, for instance, could cause an immediate need for steel. A national disaster might create a sudden need for social services. To get the money it needs, a government can raise taxes, borrow, or print more currency. However, raising taxes and borrowing are not always plausible options.*

Analysis: The paragraph starts with a definition and proceeds to examine a causal chain. The words *consequently, reasons,* and *cause* provide the clues.

Explicit Cause and Effect

General Hooker failed to anticipate General Lee's bold flanking maneuver. As a result, Hooker's army was nearly routed by a smaller force.

Mindy forgot to bring the lunch her father had packed for her. Consequently, she had to borrow money from her friends at school during lunch period.

Implicit Cause and Effect

The engine in Lisa's airplane began to sputter. She quickly looked below for a field in which to land. Luther ate the creamed shrimp that had been sitting in the sun for hours. Later that night, he was so sick he had to be rushed to the hospital.

Whenever there are two ideas in opposition, there is the ghost of an "either/or" conceptual basis lurking invisibly in the background of the "pro/con" setting.

For example, one person may argue that automobiles are a safer mode of transportation than are motorcycles and support that contention with statistics showing that fatalities are more frequent per accident in motorcycle crashes than in car crashes.

An **inference** is sometimes called an *educated guess* because it requires that you go beyond the strictly obvious to create additional meaning by taking the text one logical step further. Inferences and conclusions are based on the content of the passage—that is, on what the passage says or how the writer says it—and are derived by reasoning. Inference is an essential and automatic component of most reading. Examples include making educated guesses about the meaning of unknown words, the author's main idea, or the presence of bias in his or her writing. Such is the essence of inference—you use your own ability to reason in order to figure out what the writer implies. As a reader, then, you must often logically extend meaning that is only implied.

Consider the following example. Assume you are an employer, and you are reading over the letters of reference submitted by a prospective employee for the position of clerk/typist in your real estate office. The position requires the applicant to be neat, careful, trustworthy, and punctual. You come across this letter of reference submitted by an applicant.

> *To Whom It May Concern:*
>
> *Todd Finley has asked me to write a letter of reference for him. I am well qualified to do so because he worked for me for three months last year. His duties included answering the phone, greeting the public, and producing some simple memos and notices on the computer. Although Todd initially had few computer skills and little knowledge of telephone etiquette, he did acquire some during his stay with us. Todd's manner of speaking, both on the telephone and with the clients who came to my establishment, could be described as casual. He was particularly effective when communicating with peers. Please contact me by telephone if you wish to have further information about my experience with Todd.*

Here the writer implies, rather than openly states, the main idea. This letter calls attention to itself because there is a problem with its tone. A truly positive letter would say something such as, "I have the distinct honor of recommending Todd Finley." Here, however, the letter simply verifies that Todd worked in the office. Second, the praise is obviously lukewarm. For example, the writer says that Todd "was particularly effective when communicating with peers." An educated guess translates that statement into a nice way of saying Todd was not serious about his communication with clients.

In order to draw **inferences** and make **conclusions**, a reader must use prior knowledge and apply it to the current situation. A conclusion or inference is never stated. You must rely on your common sense.

Practice Questions: Read the following passages and select an answer.

1. Tim Sullivan had just turned fifteen. As a birthday present, his parents had given him a guitar and a certificate for ten guitar lessons. He had always shown a love of music and a desire to learn an instrument. Tim began his lessons, and before long, he was making up his own songs. At the music studio, Tim met Josh, who played the piano, and Roger, whose instrument was the saxophone. They all shared the same dream, to start a band, and each was praised by his teacher as having real talent.

    From this passage, one can infer that

    A. Tim, Roger, and Josh are going to start their own band.
    B. Tim is going to give up his guitar lessons.
    C. Tim, Josh, and Roger will no longer be friends.
    D. Josh and Roger are going to start their own band.

2. The Smith family waited patiently around carousel number 7 for their luggage to arrive. They were exhausted after their five-hour trip and were anxious to get to their hotel. After about an hour, they realized that they no longer recognized any of the other passengers' faces. Mrs. Smith asked the person who appeared to be in charge if they were at the right carousel. The man replied, "Yes, this is it, but we finished unloading that baggage almost half an hour ago."

    From the man's response, we can infer that

    A. The Smiths were ready to go to their hotel.
    B. The Smiths' luggage was lost.
    C. The man had their luggage.
    D. They were at the wrong carousel.

Answers:

1. A is the correct choice. Given the facts that Tim wanted to be a musician and start his own band, after meeting others who shared the same dreams, we can infer that they joined in an attempt to make their dreams become a reality.

2. Since the Smiths were still waiting for their luggage, we know that they were not yet ready to go to their hotel. From the man's response, we know that they were not at the wrong carousel and that he did not have their luggage. Therefore, though not directly stated, it appears that their luggage was lost. Choice B is the correct answer.

Facts and Opinions

Facts are verifiable statements. Opinions are statements, such as beliefs, values, judgments, or feelings, which must be supported in order to be accepted, Facts are objective statements used to support subjective opinions. For example, "Jane is a bad girl" is an opinion. However, "Jane hit her sister with a baseball bat" is a *fact* upon which the opinion is based. Judgments are opinions—decisions or declarations based on observation or reasoning—that express approval or disapproval. Facts report what has happened or exists and come from observation, measurement, or calculation. Facts can be tested and verified, whereas opinions and judgments cannot. They can only be supported with facts.

Most statements cannot be so clearly distinguished. "I believe that Jane is a bad girl" is a fact. The speaker knows what he/she believes. However, it obviously includes a judgment that could be disputed by another person who might believe otherwise. Judgments are not usually so firm. They are, rather, plausible opinions that provoke thought or lead to factual development.

Mickey Mantle replaced Joe DiMaggio, a Yankees' centerfielder, in 1952.

This is a fact. If necessary, evidence can be produced to support this.

First year players are more ambitious than seasoned players are.
This is an opinion. There is no proof to support that everyone feels this way.

Practice Questions: Decide if the statement is fact or opinion.

1. The Inca were a group of Indians who ruled an empire in South America.

   (A) fact
   (B) opinion

2. The Inca were clever.

   (A) fact
   (B) opinion

3. The Inca built very complex systems of bridges.

   (A) fact
   (B) opinion

Answers:

1. A is the correct answer. Research can prove this true.
2. B is the correct answer. It is doubtful that all people who have studied the Inca agree with this statement. Therefore, no proof is available.
3. A is the correct answer. As with question number one, research can prove this true.

Summarizing

One way to determine the understanding of your students is to have them summarize a passage. To do so, they must be able to determine the main ideas and supporting details and then identify the underlying structure.

Summary skills can be developed through practice and repetition. Here's an example:

Sample Passage

Chili peppers may turn out to be the wonder drug of the decade. The fiery fruit comes in many sizes, shapes, and colors, all of which grow on plants that are genetic descendants of the tepin plant, originally native to the Americas. Connoisseurs of the regional cuisines of the Southwest and Louisiana are already well aware that food flavored with chilies can cause a good sweat, but medical researchers are learning more every day about the medical power of capsaicin, the ingredient in the peppers that produces the heat.

Capsaicin as a pain medication has been a part of old medicine for centuries. It is, in fact, the active ingredient in several currently available over-the-counter liniments for sore muscles. Recent research has been examining the value of the compound for the treatment of other painful conditions. Capsaicin shows some promise in the treatment of phantom limb syndrome, as well as shingles and some types of headaches.

Additional research focuses upon the use of capsaicin to relieve pain in post-surgical patients. Scientists speculate that application of the compound to the skin causes the body to release endorphins—natural pain relievers manufactured by the body itself. An alternative theory holds that capsaicin somehow interferes with the transmission of signals along the nerve fibers, thus reducing the sensation of pain.

In addition to its well-documented history as a painkiller, capsaicin has recently received attention as a phytochemical, one of the naturally occurring compounds from foods that show cancer-fighting qualities. Like the phytochemical sulfoaphane found in broccoli, capsaicin might turn out to be an agent capable of short-circuiting the actions of carcinogens at the cell level before they can cause cancer.

Summary: Chili peppers contain a chemical called capsaicin, which has proved useful for treating a variety of ailments. Recent research reveals that capsaicin is a phytochemical, a natural compound that may help fight cancer

0009 Understand reading comprehension strategies for fiction and poetry.

Authors use various methods to tell a story while employing various literary techniques. If teachers want students to understand the technique, they need to teach them the characteristics of each narrative genre. It may be necessary to draw the students' attention to the elements and structure of narratives as well to the strategies they can use for reading each of the genres. Before students actually read a selection, the teacher can prepare students by addressing relevant literary techniques, writing forms, and vocabulary in mini-lessons to provide the students with knowledge about what they will be reading. This helps students to become more engaged with the text and to have an idea of what they should think about as they are reading.

Narrative Genres

Prose Fiction
This is literature about imaginary people, places, and events. The purpose of this narrative genre is to stimulate the students' imaginations and to present the author's view of the world. This genre includes novels, short stories, and plays, each of which has its own distinctive characteristics. They all have a setting, conflict, plot, climax, and resolution, to varying degrees.

Short Story
This narrative usually has only one focus and a smaller world view. The students do have to determine whether the person telling the story is a narrator or is a character within the story. They do have to take note of the central conflict and determine why the characters act as they do. As a response to the story, they can decide how they feel about the characters and their actions and ask questions about the message the author is trying to convey in the story.

Novel
A novel is a longer version of the short story, often with sub-plots. During the reading the students have to be able to keep the subplots separated and understand their relationship to the main plot of the novel. They must be aware of the motives of the various characters and of their reactions to the characters' actions.

Prose Non-fiction

This is literature that is about real events, times, and places. It includes essays, journals, articles, letters, biographies, and autobiographies. Much of contemporary nonfiction reads like fiction with suspense, expression, and ingenuity of style. Because it is vivid and personal, it can provide the students with a model for their own writing. When students are reading for information, they need to keep this purpose in mind and may need time and instruction to help them summarize or restate the main ideas.

Poetry

In this form of literature, the author communicates ideas and feelings through composition written in verse. Poetry can be used to capture a mood, tell a story, or explore different ideas. There are various literary techniques authors use in writing poetry which the teacher can discuss with the class through mini-lessons.

Plays

These can be read for the purpose of performance or for literary effect. Students pay attention to the literary devices that the author uses. When reading a play, students can work on putting expression into their reading so that they can bring the characters to life.

Types of Text

There are six different types of texts that are usually used in a school setting. Each type of text has a specific use within the classroom depending on the purpose for reading set forth by the teacher. The *types* of texts vary from the *genres* of reading and should not be confused.

Wordless Books

Wordless picture books are generally used to increase discussion and develop vocabulary. These books are good for generating ideas for writing or discussions among students. They provide pictures filled with details to serve as a springboard to oral language development or increasing the quality of description in writing.

Predictable Texts

Predictable texts allow the beginning reader to feel rapid success with the process of reading. They provide the same words or phrases repeated over and over so that students can participate in the act of reading. They are also generally very much enjoyed by students due to the natural rhythm that develops by the repetitions. However, this type of text should be moved through rapidly so that children begin to attend to the words in reading and not rely on their auditory memory alone for what comes next.

Controlled Vocabulary Texts

Texts of this nature are usually used to increase student vocabulary with the use of high-frequency words. This sight word reading vocabulary is critical to later success with more advanced reading tasks. This type of book generally has a very slim plot or story line and is more beneficial for word recall than for building comprehension.

Decodable Texts

Decodable texts are comprised of specific phonics skills. There is usually a range of these books spanning a great many different phonics skills. The stories are usually progressive as the skills learned in earlier books are reinforced in later books. As with controlled vocabulary texts, these books rarely have well developed story lines and are not well suited to comprehension development. They do, however, have a significant place in helping students unlock the code to reading.

Authentic Literature

This is the type of reading that most people are familiar with and is the typical goal of all reading. All children should have the experience of reading authentic literature and real stories. These can be fiction or nonfiction but provide numerous details and allow for the development of comprehension skills. They range in difficulty and length, but are at the core of reading.

Created, Easy-to-Read Texts

This last text type would encompass teacher-created reading passages or books to fill a specific purpose within the curriculum for all or a group of students.

Students should be aware of the purpose for reading so they know what thinking is expected of them. When reading any text, students need to employ certain strategies. Therefore teachers need to engage the students in the reading process and model the appropriate strategies of:

- Connecting
- Making meaning
- Questioning
- Predicting
- Inferring
- Reflecting
- Evaluating

In fiction, writers use various elements to gain reader interest. The elements a fiction author uses in developing the narrative include:

- Plot
- Character
- Setting
- Theme

When readers understand these elements, they will have a greater understanding and appreciation for the fictional text. These elements help readers to segment the story and blend the story into a whole. The knowledge of these elements is necessary for readers to be able to discuss and respond to the text.

Plot

Plot is an attribute shared by novels, short stories, and plays. Plot is *not* the same thing as *story*. *Story* is merely a synopsis of the temporal order of what happens in a narrative, while *plot* is the events and actions in the narrative performed by its character. Usually, the plot develops from the conflicts in the story. There are several different types of conflict that can be found within a work of fiction including

- Person versus person—external conflict that develops among two or more characters
- Person versus self—internal conflict in which a character is torn with regards to his/her feelings, actions, beliefs, or emotions
- Person versus nature—external conflict in which a character battles the forces of nature

The plot develops as the character makes choices and decisions affecting the outcome of the story. Complications can also develop in the plot which are the twists and turns that keep the readers captivated. Other elements of plot include:

- Rising action—the series of events leading up to the turning point of the story
- Climax—the turning point where the conflict is just about to be resolved
- Falling action—the way the conflicts are resolved bringing the story to a close.

Character

The characters in a story are an integral part of the plot. It is through the author's words that the reader comes to know the characters, their thoughts, feelings, and the reasons they act the way they do. The reader can also learn what the characters looks like because the author offers a description through the words of the text.

There are various types of characters in any fictional text. There is usually a protagonist who is the main character, and an antagonist who is in conflict with the protagonist. Characters can also be round or flat. A round character is one that is fully developed in the story and is often prone to change. A flat character is usually a one-dimensional character not central to the story line.

The author reveals the characters by showing their thoughts and actions through words and by telling what others think and say about them.

Setting

The setting is where the story takes place. There can be several different settings in one story. The author describes the setting of the story by using imagery and colorful words in order to give the reader a visual representation of the area. The setting can also be a time period which is important to understanding why and how the characters act the way they do.

Theme

The theme of a story is the central message the author wished to convey. Sometimes the theme may be directly stated and at other times, it may be inferred through the thoughts and actions of the character(s). It can be a revelation into the insight of people in general, or an opinion on a way of life. It is not, however, the moral of the story. There are certain requirements for an idea to be the central theme of a text:

> 1. It must be related to all the elements of the story.

> 2. It cannot be contradicted by any details presented in the story.

It has to be supported by evidence from the text.

Within the assessment of reading, working with more than one selection is important in deciding if students can generalize. Utilizing the information read to find the answer to a situation presented is the skill. Sometimes this may involve problems specifically identified within what was read. For example, the characters in the story may be having a specific problem, such as a lack of money. Then, as you continue to read the passage, the characters in the story were hired for a new job, which allowed them to earn more money. Using the information read, identify the problem (a lack of money) and the solution (a new job).

In other cases, generalizations will need to be made across multiple selections. In those cases, selecting problems and solutions may be more evasive. Problems and solutions across texts will require broader thinking. The problems and solutions will not be as clearly spelled out in the text. It will involve your thinking on a different level about how the two passages relate. Connecting texts to other texts and finding common elements within them allows you then to draw out the common problems and solutions. Working through multiple selections requires more complex thinking skills and thinking of problems and solutions sometimes in other terms. Perhaps thinking of the challenge or issue that was faced and how that issue was overcome would help to broaden the scope and understanding of identifying the common problem and therefore the solution.

Figurative Language

1. **Simile**: Direct comparison between two things. For example, "My love is like a red-red rose."
2. **Metaphor**: Indirect comparison between two things; the use of a word or phrase denoting one kind of object or action in place of another to suggest a comparison between them. While poets use them extensively, they are also integral to everyday speech. For example, chairs are said to have "legs" and "arms," although we know that it is humans and other animals that have these appendages.
3. **Parallelism**: The arrangement of ideas in phrases, sentences, and paragraphs that balance one element with another of equal importance and similar wording. An example from Francis Bacon's *Of Studies:* "Reading maketh a full man, conference a ready man, and writing an exact man."
4. **Personification**: Human characteristics are attributed to an inanimate object, an abstract quality, or animal. Examples: John Bunyan wrote characters named Death, Knowledge, Giant Despair, Sloth, and Piety in his *Pilgrim's Progress*. The metaphor of an arm of a chair is a form of personification.
5. **Euphemism**: The substitution of an agreeable or inoffensive term for one that might offend or suggest something unpleasant. Many euphemisms, such as *passed away, crossed over*, or nowadays, *passed*, are used to refer to death to avoid using the real word.
6. **Hyperbole**: Deliberate exaggeration for effect or comic effect. An example from Shakespeare's *The Merchant of Venice*:
   > Why, if two gods should play some heavenly match
   > And on the wager lay two earthly women,
   > And Portia one, there must be something else
   > Pawned with the other, for the poor rude world
   > Hath not her fellow.
7. **Climax**: A number of phrases or sentences are arranged in ascending order of rhetorical forcefulness. Example from Melville's *Moby Dick*:
   > All that most maddens and torments; all that stirs up the lees of things; all truth with malice in it; all that cracks the sinews and cakes the brain; all the subtle demonisms of life and thought; all evil, to crazy Ahab, were visibly personified and made practically assailable in Moby Dick.

8. <u>**Bathos**</u>: A ludicrous attempt to portray pathos—that is, to evoke pity, sympathy, or sorrow. It may result from inappropriately dignifying the commonplace, elevated language to describe something trivial, or greatly exaggerated pathos.

9. <u>**Oxymoron**</u>: A contradiction in terms deliberately employed for effect. It is usually seen in a qualifying adjective whose meaning is contrary to that of the noun it modifies, such as wise folly.

10. <u>**Irony**</u>: Expressing something other than and particularly opposite of the literal meaning, such as words of praise when blame is intended. In poetry, it is often used as a sophisticated or resigned awareness of contrast between what is and what ought to be and expresses a controlled pathos without sentimentality. This form of indirection avoids overt praise or censure. An early example is the Greek comic character Eiron, a clever underdog who by his wit repeatedly triumphs over the boastful character Alazon.

11. <u>**Alliteration**</u>: The repetition of consonant sounds in two or more neighboring words or syllables. In its simplest form, it reinforces one or two consonant sounds. Example: Shakespeare's Sonnet #12: When I do count the clock that tells the time. Some poets have used patterns of alliteration that are more complex by creating consonants both at the beginning of words and at the beginning of stressed syllables within words. For example, Shelley's *Stanzas Written in Dejection near Naples*: The City's voice itself is soft like Solitude's.

12. <u>**Onomatopoeia**</u>: The naming of a thing or action by a vocal imitation of the sound associated with it, such as *buzz* or *hiss* or the use of words whose sound suggests the sense. A good example is from *The Brook* by Tennyson:

> I chatter over stony ways,
> In little sharps and trebles,
> I bubble into eddying bays,
> I babble on the pebbles.

0010 Understand reading comprehension strategies for nonfiction.

Reading comprehension is the ultimate goal of any reading activity. As students progress through the grades, it becomes increasingly important that they be able to read factual information in the content areas, like science and social studies, with as much efficiency and solid comprehension. So much learning and teaching occurs through the use of texts that students need to be taught specific methods to gain comprehension from these books.

Typically, content-area texts are nonfiction in nature. Therefore, students can use specific strategies to help gain more insight. First, students can begin by analyzing the text itself. Looking at the organization and layout of the text can provide:

1. Cues students may use to filter out their need to read nonpertinent information.

2. Pointers to the specific places in the text where the answers sought may be located

3. Additional ways to connect information to prior knowledge, thus making the content more meaningful.

This analysis of text structure is a critical skill for students to achieve.

Additionally, the texts generally will have large amounts of information to convey. This can be overwhelming to students. Students will need some sort of organizational tool to absorb the necessary information. Using *summarizing skills,* the students can break the information and into smaller, more manageable pieces.

Another beneficial tool for students is *semantic mapping.* In semantic mapping, students begin to make the connections between the information they already know about the topic and the new information they are learning. It is typically a more graphic representation of the information, but it is built upon words and ideas. Mapping generally increases knowledge and improves vocabulary development.

Other types of graphic organizers can also help students acquire information from content area texts. Mind mapping, for example, is a strategy that combines pictures and words to convey the underlying concepts of what was read. There are many different types of graphic organizers from which a teacher can draw to support students. However, students need to be able to apply these skills on their own. In other words, they need to be able to create their own graphic organizer to meet the needs of the task before them. A personally created organizer can become the most efficient and most meaningful strategy of all.

As previously discussed, one of the most important thing to improve reading comprehension is to help students understand how the new information relates to information they have already. Using prior knowledge and experiences can make the difference between what is remembered and what is forgotten.

Making learning as real as possible with real-life practical applications is one strategy to increase students' use of prior knowledge. If the students are learning about adding money and discounts, try relating that information to shopping for clothes that are "cool". This real-life application automatically engages the student in recalling prior knowledge while staying interested in the current lesson in the classroom.

Another strategy for helping students tap prior knowledge is to use *Know, Wonder, Learn* (KWL). Students typically already have some information about topics being discussed in class. When the students share that prior knowledge, either as individuals or in a group, the teacher is able to point out specific connections. Although there are many different forms of the KWL chart, the one below is the simplest.

Know	Wonder	Learn
In this box, the teacher or students list the information they already know about the topic to be discussed	In this box, the teacher or students list the questions they have about the topic, which may be answered through research or the activities already planned to be completed	In this box, the teacher or students list what information has been learned at the *end* of the teaching process. This becomes a nice reflective piece for both students and teachers, and can even be used as a quick assessment for the teacher to whether ascertain all predetermined objectives were met

Essay

An essay is a short work of nonfiction giving the author's opinion on a specific topic. While nonfiction essays are expository, they also tend to be subjective and can include narrative. Essays can also be literary criticism, political manifestos, arguments, observations, or even personal reflections. Quite often the first exposure students have to an essay is the five paragraph essay, which consists of an introductory paragraph, three paragraphs about the topic and a concluding paragraph. There are also different types of academic essays:

- Descriptive—provides a vivid picture of a location, person, object, event, or debate
- Narrative—tells a story as a way of presenting a point of view or opinion on a topic
- Compare and contrast —develops the relationship between two or more objects
- Persuasive—attempts to persuade the reader to accept or agree with an idea or a point of view
- Argumentative—argues one side of an issue, giving supporting evidence

Biography

A biography is a written account of a person's life. It usually highlights specific aspects of personality, gives insight into events in the person's life, and often includes intimate details that are not widely known. A biography is written about a person by a different author and, because of this, is written from the third person point of view.

Autobiography

An autobiography is an account of a person's life written by that person. When one is telling about one's life, the opinions expressed may be biased as the author is telling about his/her own life. Therefore events may be exaggerated or events may be omitted. It is written from the first person point of view.

Memoir

A memoir is a type of autobiography, but usually deals with only one or two aspects of the author's life. It is not as structured as an autobiography because it is usually about only one portion of the author's life rather than the entire life. Like the autobiography, a memoir is usually written from the first person point of view.

Editorial

An editorial is a statement or a news article written by a news organization. It expresses the opinion of the editor, editorial board, or the publisher on topics of interest to the readers. They often address current events or public controversies. Such writing is usually short, and is always labeled an editorial. There is no byline, but it does say that the information contained in the piece is the opinion of the writer and does not reflect that of the organization as a whole.

Textbook

A textbook presents information for the formal study of a subject area and includes many different topics. The book is divided into chapters, each one focusing on a specific topic. There are many features in a textbook, such as a table of contents, index, and glossary, along with photos, charts, maps, and diagrams.

News Article

A news article presents factual information usually about recent events or happenings or on an item of interest to the readers. Fundamental to these writing is answering the Five Ws (*Who? What? When? Where?* and *Why?*) and *How?* News articles may be accompanied by photos or illustrations.

Textual Features

To make the most of their reading experiences, students need to know the various features of texts that can help them understand the material. These include:

- **Paragraphs**—Ideas are arranged into paragraphs with each paragraph centered around one main idea. There is a beginning sentence, three or four supporting sentences and a concluding sentence. The *topic sentence* is usually the first sentence, but it can be anywhere in the paragraph. All the other sentences are designed to provide more information about the topic sentence. They give details, reasons, and examples to support the topic. The *concluding sentence* brings closure to the paragraph and restates the main point of the paragraph.

- **Glossary**—This section of a text provides definitions for words in the text. Throughout the text, words included in the glossary are written in bold type so that they are easily identified.

- **Graphic Features**—Some of the graphic features included in texts are maps, charts, diagrams, and illustrations designed to elaborate on information presented in the text.

Common organizational structures of informational texts include such things as:

- **Chronological Order** —a listing of events as they happen from beginning to end.

- **Logical Order**—the physical order of the text; differs according to topic. In some informational texts the information can be arranged in alphabetical order or in order of importance.

- **Cause and Effect**—a type of informational text discussing the topic in terms of what causes it or what it causes and the effect this has on other objects or people.

Teaching children to make inferences must begin at the word level and then can be broadened to more complex concepts. From a very young age, students can evaluate the textual and picture information provided within the stories to make appropriate inferences.

It is important to remember that the process of making an inference about anything related to a story requires the reader to utilize their prior knowledge and information presented within the story to draw a conclusion. These conclusions may be unique to each student because each person's prior knowledge will be different. Therefore, it is important children understand the components of making an inference.

These components include:

- Looking back at the words/pictures

- Paying close attention to the words

- Using what they already know

- Thinking about what makes sense with what they know, see, and have read

It is important to provide children with structured opportunities to practice confirming their inferences/predictions. If they can find confirmation or contradictions, within the text, it helps them to use the information to become more strategic readers. Inferences will need to be made when students are reading and come to unknown items. It is an important skill to develop.

Main Idea
The main idea of a passage or paragraph is the basic message, idea, point concept, or meaning that the author wants to convey to you, the reader. Understanding the main idea of a passage or paragraph is the key to understanding the more subtle components of the author's message. The main idea is what is being said about a topic or subject. Once you have identified the basic message, you will have an easier time answering other questions that test critical skills.

Main ideas are either *stated* or *implied*. A *stated main idea* is explicit; it is directly expressed in a sentence or two in the paragraph or passage. An *implied main idea* is suggested by the overall reading selection. In the first case, you need not pull information from various points in the paragraph or passage in order to form the main idea because the author already states it. If a main idea is implied, however, you must formulate, in your own words, a main idea statement by condensing the overall message contained in the material itself

Practice Question: Read the following passage and select an answer.

Sometimes too much of a good thing can become a very bad thing indeed. In an earnest attempt to consume a healthy diet, dietary supplement enthusiasts have been known to overdose. Vitamin C, for example, long thought to help people ward off cold viruses, is currently being studied for its possible role in warding off cancer and other disease that causes tissue degeneration. Unfortunately, an overdose of vitamin C—more than 10 mg—on a daily basis can cause nausea and diarrhea. Calcium supplements, commonly taken by women, are helpful in warding off osteoporosis. More than just a few grams a day, however, can lead to stomach upset and even kidney and bladder stones. Niacin, proven useful in reducing cholesterol levels, can be dangerous in large doses to those who suffer from heart problems, asthma, or ulcers.

The main idea expressed in this paragraph is

A.   Supplements taken in excess can be a bad thing indeed.
B.   Dietary supplement enthusiasts have been known to overdose.
C.   Vitamins can cause nausea, diarrhea, and kidney or bladder stones.
D.   People who take supplements are preoccupied with their health.

Answer: Answer A is a paraphrase of the first sentence and provides a general framework for the rest of the paragraph—excess supplement intake is bad. The rest of the paragraph discusses the consequences of taking too many vitamins. Options B and C refer to major details and Option D introduces the idea of preoccupation, which is not included in this paragraph.

Supporting details

Supporting details are examples, facts, ideas, illustrations, cases, and anecdotes used by a writer to explain, expand on, and develop the more general main idea. A writer's choice of supporting materials is determined by the nature of the topic being covered. Supporting details are specifics that relate directly to the main idea Writers select and shape material according to their purposes. An advertisement writer seeking to persuade the reader to buy a particular running shoe, for instance, will emphasize only the positive characteristics of the shoe for advertisement copy. A columnist for a running magazine, on the other hand, might list the good and bad points about the same shoe in an article recommending appropriate shoes for different kinds of runners. Both major detail (those that directly support the main idea) and minor details (those that provide interesting, but not always essential, information) help create a well-written and fluid passage.

In the following paragraph, the sentences in **bold print** provide a skeleton of a paragraph on the benefits of recycling. The sentences in bold are generalizations, which by themselves do not explain the need to recycle. The sentences in *italics* add details to SHOW the general points in bold. Notice how the supporting details help you understand the necessity for recycling.

> **While one day recycling may become mandatory in all states, right now it is voluntary in many communities.** *Those of us who participate in recycling are amazed by how much material is recycled.* **For many communities, the blue-box recycling program has had an immediate effect.** *By just recycling glass, aluminum cans, and plastic bottles, we have reduced the volume of disposable trash by one third, thus extending the useful life of local landfills by over a decade. Imagine the difference if those dramatic results were achieved nationwide.* **The amount of reusable items we thoughtlessly dispose of is staggering.** *For example, Americans dispose of enough steel everyday to supply Detroit car manufacturers for three months. Additionally, we dispose of enough aluminum annually to rebuild the nation's air fleet. These statistics, available from the Environmental Protection Agency (EPA), should encourage all of us to watch what we throw away.* **Clearly, recycling in our homes and in our communities directly improves the environment.**

Notice how the author's supporting examples enhance the message of the paragraph and relate to the author's thesis noted above. If you only read the boldfaced sentences, you have a glimpse at the topic. This paragraph of illustration, however, is developed through numerous details creating specific images: *reduced the volume of disposable trash by one-third, extended the useful life of local landfills by over a decade, enough steel everyday to supply Detroit car manufacturers for three months, enough aluminum to rebuild the nation's air fleet.* If the writer had merely written a few general sentences, as those shown in bold print, you would not fully understand the vast amount of trash involved in recycling or the positive results of current recycling efforts.

Writer's purpose
An essay is an extended discussion of a writer's point of view about a particular topic. This point of view may be supported by using such writing modes as examples, argument and persuasion, analysis, or comparison/contrast. In any case, a good essay is clear, coherent, well organized, and fully developed.

When an author sets out to write a passage, he/she usually has a purpose for doing so. That purpose may be simply to give information that might be interesting or useful to some reader or other. It may be to persuade the reader to a point of view or to move the reader to act in a particular way. It may be to tell a story, or it may be to describe something in such a way that an experience becomes available to the reader through one of the five senses. Following are the primary devices for expressing a particular purpose in a piece of writing:

- **Basic expository writing** simply gives information not previously known about a topic or is used to explain or define one. Facts, examples, statistics, cause and effect, direct tone, objective rather than subjective delivery, and non-emotional information are presented in a formal manner.

- **Descriptive writing** centers on a person, place, or object, using concrete and sensory words to create a mood or impression and arranging details in a chronological or spatial sequence.

- **Narrative writing** is developed using an incident or anecdote or related series of events. Chronology, the five W's, topic sentence, and conclusion are essential ingredients.

- **Persuasive writing** implies the writer's ability to select vocabulary and arrange facts and opinions in such a way as to direct the actions of the listener/reader. Persuasive writing may incorporate exposition and narration as they illustrate the main idea.

- **Journalistic writing** is theoretically free of author bias. It is essential that it be factual and objective when relaying information about an event, person, or thing. Provide students with an opportunity to examine newspapers and create their own. Many newspapers have educational programs that are offered free to schools.

.Outlines

In outline information, it is crucial to identify the headings and subheadings for the topic. When researching information, it is easier to cut and paste information under the indicated headings in creating a visual flow of information for the report. In the actual drafting of the report, the writer is able to lift direct quotations and citations from the posted information to incorporate in the writing.

Sample Passage

Chili peppers may turn out to be the wonder drug of the decade. The fiery fruit comes in many sizes, shapes, and colors, all of which grow on plants that are genetic descendants of the tepin plant, originally native to the Americas. Connoisseurs of the regional cuisines of the Southwest and Louisiana are already well aware that food flavored with chilies can cause a good sweat, but medical researchers are learning more every day about the medical power of capsaicin, the ingredient in the peppers that produces the heat.

Capsaicin as a pain medication has been a part of old medicine for centuries. It is, in fact, the active ingredient in several currently available over-the-counter liniments for sore muscles. Recent research has been examining the value of the compound for the treatment of other painful conditions. Capsaicin shows some promise in the treatment of phantom limb syndrome, as well as shingles and some types of headaches.

Additional research focuses upon the use of capsaicin to relieve pain in post-surgical patients. Scientists speculate that application of the compound to the skin causes the body to release endorphins—natural pain relievers manufactured by the body itself. An alternative theory holds that capsaicin somehow interferes with the transmission of signals along the nerve fibers, thus reducing the sensation of pain.

In addition to its well-documented history as a painkiller, capsaicin has recently received attention as a phytochemical, one of the naturally occurring compounds from foods that show cancer-fighting qualities. Like the phytochemical sulfoaphane found in broccoli, capsaicin might turn out to be an agent capable of short-circuiting the actions of carcinogens at the cell level before they can cause cancer.

Using the passage above, this informal outline identifies the main idea and supporting details.

Outline: -Chili peppers could be the wonder drug of the decade.
              -Chili peppers contain capsaicin.
              -Capsaicin can be used as a pain medication.
              -Capsaicin is a phytochemical.
              -Phytochemicals show cancer-fighting qualities.
              -Capsaicin might be able to short-circuit the effects of carcinogens.

Mapping

Mapping is a strategy that can be used to reach all learning styles, and therefore is an important one to teach. It is exactly what its name implies—a map of the reading. A map helps the reader maneuver through the information in a meaningful manner. Maps can use words with key ideas connected to smaller chunks of information. Teachers can also encourage pictures instead of words to help the visual learner. Adding color to a map can help certain ideas stand out more. This can be particularly helpful for students to begin to understand the process of prioritization in skills. Combining words and pictures is probably the most commonly used type of map. Lines are drawn between connecting concepts to show relationships, and because the reader is creating it himself or herself, it is meaningful. Maps are individual creations and revolve around the reader's learning and prior knowledge.

Visuals are an effective and dynamic way to add meaning to a text. They can clarify meaning, emphasize important data, summarize points, and add visual appeal. More often, they supplement the written text rather than stand independent. Learning how to interpret the data in various graphics is an important skill for students.

Some possibilities for the analysis of data whether presented in tables, charts, graphs, maps, or other illustrations are as follow:

- Qualitative descriptions: Would drawing conclusions about the quality of a particular treatment or course of action be revealed by the illustration?
- Quantitative descriptions: How much do the results of one particular treatment or course of action differ from another one, and is that variation significant?
- Classification: Is worthwhile information derived from breaking the information down into classifications?
- Estimations: Is it possible to estimate future performance on the basis of the information in the illustration?
- Comparisons: Is it useful to make comparisons based on the data?
- Relationships. Are relationships between components revealed by the scrutiny of the data?
- Cause-and-effect relationships: Is it suggested by the data that there were cause-and-effect relationships that were not previously apparent?
- Mapping and modeling: If the data were mapped and a model drawn up, would the point of the document be demonstrated or refuted?

Questions to ask regarding an illustration: Why is it in this document? What was the writer's purpose in putting it in the document and why at this particular place? Does it make a point clearer? What implications are inherent in a table that shows birth statistics in all states or even in some selected states? What does that have to do with the point and purpose of this piece of writing? Is there adequate preparation in the text for the inclusion of the illustration? Does the illustration underscore or clarify any of the points made in the text? Is there a clear connection between the illustration and the subject matter of the text?

DOMAIN IV. WRITING AND RESEARCH

0011 Understand Writing skills and processes.

Because students typically write for their instructor, they have a narrow view of audience. They must learn to adapt their communication to the needs of their audiences. One way to teach this is to have students determine the values, needs, constraints, and demographics of their audience.

Values: What is important to this group of people? What is their background and how will that affect their perception of your speech?

Needs: Find out in advance what the audience's needs are. Why are they listening to you? Find a way to satisfy their needs.

Constraints: What might hold the audience back from being fully engaged in what you are saying, or agreeing with your point of view, or processing what you are trying to say? These could be political reasons, which make them wary of your presentation's ideology from the start, or knowledge reasons, in which the audience lacks the appropriate background information to grasp your ideas. Avoid this last constraint by staying away from technical terminology, slang, or abbreviations that may be unclear to your audience.

Demographic Information: Take the audience's size into account as well as the location of the presentation. Demographics could include age, gender, education, religion, income level and other such countable characteristics.

Start where the listeners are, and then take them where you want to go!

Just as you talk to different people in different ways so do you write in different styles and levels of formality. Students should learn that writers use different writing styles to accomplish their purposes and to reach their different audiences.

Is a **business letter** outdated? Although much business-letter writing has been relegated to E-mail communications, letters are still a valuable form of communication. A carefully written letter can be powerful. It can convince, persuade, alienate, entice, motivate, and/or create good will.

As with any other communication, you will need to know information about your receiver. This may be complicated if there will be more than one receiver of the message; in these cases, write for the largest or most important group of readers without "writing down" to any of those who will read and be affected or influenced by the letter. It may be better to send more than one form of the letter to the various receivers in some cases.

Purpose is the most powerful factor in writing a business letter. What is the letter expected to accomplish? Is it intended to motivate the receiver to act or to act in a specific manner? Are you hoping to see some action take place as the result of the letter? If so, you should clearly define for yourself what the purpose is before you craft the letter. To avoid procrastination, include time deadline for the response.

Why should you choose a letter format as your channel of communication?

1. It's easy to keep a record of the transaction.
2. The message can be edited and perfected before it is transmitted.
3. It facilitates the handling of details.
4. It's ideal for communicating complex information.
5. It's a good way to disseminate mass messages at a relatively low cost.

Because letters have external readers, they typically use formal language. They should be straightforward and courteous. The writing should be concise and complete; otherwise, more than one exchange of letters or phone calls to get the message across may be necessary.

A **complaint** is a different kind of business letter. It can come under the classification of a "bad news" business letter, and guidelines are helpful when writing this kind of letter. A positive writing style can overcome much of the inherent negativity of a letter of complaint. No matter how much in the right you may be, maintaining self-control and courtesy and avoiding demeaning or blaming language is more likely to be effective. Abruptness, condescension, or harshness of tone will not help achieve your purpose, particularly if you are requesting a positive response such as reimbursement for a bad product or some help in righting a wrong that may have been done to you. The goal is to solve the specific problem and to retain the good will of the receiver if possible.

Induction is better than deduction for this type of communication. Beginning with the details and building to the statement of the problem generally has the effect of softening the bad news. It's also useful to begin with an opening that will serve as a buffer. The same is true for the closing. Leave the reader with a favorable impression by writing a closing paragraph that will generate good will rather than bad.

E-mail has revolutionized business communications. It has most of the advantages of business letters and the added ones of immediacy, lower costs, and convenience. Even very long reports can be attached to an E-mail. On the other hand, a two-line message can be sent and a response received immediately bringing together the features of a postal system and the telephone.

Instant messaging goes even one step further. It can do all of the above—send messages, attach reports—and still have many of the advantages of a telephone conversation. E-mail has an unwritten code of behavior that includes restrictions on how informal the writing can be. The level of accepted business conversation is usually also acceptable in E-mails. Capital letters and bolding are considered shouting and are usually frowned on.

Remind students that e-mail messages, even if intended for just one reader, may eventually reach a much wider audience. In recent years, a number of e-mail writers have found themselves in embarrassing situations or legal troubles because of the circulation of their personal e-mails on the Internet. When writers need to address a sensitive, unpleasant or controversial matter, they should consult state laws to determine whether personal privacy laws protect correspondence. If the law does protect such correspondence from being circulated by the addressee, then the writers may wish to mention this in their messages to forestall publication. Otherwise, clarity, concision, and civility in written works will protect writers.

Personal Letters

When writing personal notes or letters, the writer needs to keep the following key matters in mind:

- Once the topic is determined, the writer must determine the appropriate tone to introduce and express it. Is humor appropriate? Seriousness? Bluntness or subtlety? Does the situation call for formal or informal language? The answers to these questions will depend, in good part, on the writer's relationship to the reader. Plan appropriately regarding situation and audience.
- Does the writer's introduction clearly explain the topic/situation to a reader who doesn't know or feel what the reader knows or feels? Don't assume that the writer and reader are the same mindset. Use a checklist to make sure all key information is clearly and concisely expressed.
- If a note or letter involves a request, what type of response/result does the writer desire? Devise a strategy or strategies for achieving a desired outcome.
- If a note or letter involves a complaint about the reader, the writer will need to decide whether to ask for particular amends or to let the reader decide what, if anything, to do. If no amends are requested, the writer may wish to suggest ideas that would help to avoid similar conflicts in the future. Asking the reader for his or her opinions is also a possibility.

- If a timely response to any note or letter is needed, the writer must mention this.

Provide students in-class opportunities to write a variety of personal notes and letters, whether involving real life or hypothetical situations. Invitations, thank-you notes, complaints, requests for favors, or personal updates are a few of the options available. Have students experiment with a variety of tones and strategies on a particular piece of personal correspondence. For example, they could write a complaint letter in a blunt tone, then write the same complaint in a humorous tone; compare and contrast the drafts. Structure in-class activities to allow for peer feedback.

Types of Persuasive Speech

1. **Fact**: Similar to an informative speech, a persuasive speech on a question of fact seeks to find an answer where there isn't a clear one. The speaker evaluates evidence and attempts to convince the audience that their conclusion is correct. The challenge is to accept a certain carefully crafted view of the facts presented.

2. **Value**: This kind of persuasion tries to convince the audience that a certain thing is good or bad, moral or immoral, valuable or worthless. It focuses less on knowledge and more on beliefs and values.

3. **Policy**: This speech is a call to action, arguing that something should be done, improved, or changed. Its goal is action from the audience, but it also seeks passive agreement with the proposition proposed. It appeals to both reason and emotion, and tells listeners what they can do and how to do it.

Tailoring language for a particular **audience** is an important skill. Writing to be read by a business associate will surely sound different from writing to be read by a younger sibling. Not only are the vocabularies different, but the formality/informality of the discourse will also need to be adjusted.

Determining what the language should be for a particular audience, then, hinges on two things: **word choice** and **formality/informality**. The most formal language does not use contractions or slang. The most informal language will probably feature a more casual use of common sayings and anecdotes. Formal language will use longer sentences and will not sound like a conversation. The most informal language will use shorter sentences—not necessarily simple sentences, but shorter constructions—and may sound like a conversation.

In both formal and informal writing, there exists a **tone**, the writer's attitude toward the material and/or readers. Tone may be playful, formal, intimate, angry, serious, ironic, outraged, baffled, tender, serene, depressed, and so on. Both the subject matter and the audience dictate the overall tone of a piece of writing. Tone is also related to the actual words that make up the document, as we attach affective meanings to words, called **connotations**. Gaining this conscious control over language makes it possible to use language appropriately in various situations and to evaluate its uses in literature and other forms of communication.

By evoking the proper responses from readers/listeners, we can prompt them to take action.

The following questions are an excellent way to assess the audience and tone of a given piece of writing.

1. Who is your audience? (friend, teacher, business person, someone else)
2. How much does this person know about you and/or your topic?
3. What is your purpose? (to prove an argument, to persuade, to amuse, to register a complaint, to ask for a raise, etc.)
4. What emotions do you have about the topic? (nervous, happy, confident, angry, sad, no feelings at all)
5. What emotions do you want to register with your audience? (anger, nervousness, happiness, boredom, interest)
6. What persona do you need to create in order to achieve your purpose?
7. What choice of language is best suited to achieving your purpose with your particular subject? (slang, friendly but respectful, formal)
8. What emotional quality do you want to transmit to achieve your purpose (matter of fact, informative, authoritative, inquisitive, sympathetic, or angry) and to what degree do you want to express this tone?

Paragraphs should contain concrete, interesting information and supporting details to support the main idea or point of view. Fact statements add weight to opinions, especially when the writer is trying to convince the reader of his or her viewpoint. Because every good thesis has an assertion, a well-written passage offers specifics, facts, data, anecdotes, expert opinion, and other details to *show* or *prove* that assertion. While *the author* knows what he or she wants to convey, the *reader* does not.

Like a whole piece of writing, the paragraphs that make up that piece can take a number of forms or combinations of forms. These forms help create an organized and well-structured document:

Cause-and-effect is used to show the reasons for the result of some action.

Compare-and-contrast is used to show similarities and differences between two or more items.

Definition is used if a simple dictionary definition is not sufficient.

Example and illustration is used to show a point by citing examples.

Sequence and process is used to show a step-by-step procedure.

A piece of writing should end with a brief straightforward **concluding paragraph** that ties together the written content and leaves the reader with a sense of its completion. The conclusion should reinforce the main points and offer some insight into the topic, provide a sense of unity for the essay by relating it to the thesis, and signal clear closure of the essay.

Even if the sentences that make up a given paragraph or passage are arranged in logical order, the document as a whole can still seem choppy, the various ideas disconnected. **Transitions**, words that signal relationships between ideas, can help improve the flow of a document. Transitions can help achieve clear and effective presentation of information by establishing connections between sentences, paragraphs, and sections of a document. With transitions, each sentence builds on the ideas in the last, and each paragraph has clear links to the preceding one. As a result, the reader receives clear directions on how to piece together the writer's ideas in a logically coherent argument. By signaling how to organize, interpret, and react to information, transitions allow a writer to explain his or her ideas effectively and elegantly.

Logical Relationship	**Transitional Expression**
Similiarity	aiso, in the same way, just as ... so too, likewise, similarly
Exception/Contrast	but, however, in spite of, on the one hand ... on the other hand, nevertheless, nonetheless, notwithstanding, in contrast, on the contrary, still, yet
Sequence/Order	first, second, third, ... next, then, finally
Time	after, afterward, at last, before, currently, during, earlier, immediately, later, meanwhile, now, recently, simultaneously, subsequently, then
Example	for example, for instance, namely, specifically, to illustrate
Emphasis	even, indeed, in fact, of course, truly
Place/Position	above, adjacent, below, beyond, here, in front, in back, nearby, there
Cause and Effect	accordingly, consequently, hence, so, therefore, thus
Additional Support or Evidence	additionally, again, also, and, as well, besides, equally important, further, furthermore, in addition, moreover, then
Conclusion/Summary	finally, in a word, in brief, in conclusion, in the end, in the final analysis, on the whole, thus, to conclude, to summarize, in sum, in summary

The following example shows good logical order and transitions, with the transition words being highlighted.

No one really knows how Valentine's Day started. There are several legends, **however**, which are often told. The **first** attributes Valentine's Day to a Christian priest who lived in Rome during the third century, under the rule of Emperor Claudius. Rome was at war, and **apparently,** Claudius felt that married men did not fight as well as bachelors. **Consequently**, Claudius banned marriage for the duration of the war. **However,** Valentinus, the priest, risked his life to marry couples secretly in violation of Claudius' law. The **second** legend is **even more** romantic. **In this story**, Valentinus is a prisoner, having been condemned to death for refusing to worship pagan deities. **While** in jail, he fell in love with his jailer's daughter, who happened to be blind. Daily, he prayed for her sight to return, and miraculously it did. On February 14, the day that he was condemned to die, he was allowed to write the young woman a note. **In this farewell letter**, he promised eternal love, and signed at the bottom of the page the now famous words, "Your Valentine."

Sentence structure

Recognize simple, compound, complex, and compound-complex sentences. Use dependent (subordinate) and independent clauses correctly to create these sentence structures.

Simple—Consists of one independent clause.
> *Joyce wrote a letter.*

Compound—Consists of two or more independent clauses. The two clauses are usually connected by a coordinating conjunction (and, but, or, nor, for, so, yet). Semicolons sometimes connect compound sentences.
> *Joyce wrote a letter and Dot drew a picture.*

Complex—Consists of an independent clause plus one or more dependent clauses. The dependent clause may precede the independent clause or follow it.
> *While Joyce wrote a letter, Dot drew a picture.*

Compound/Complex—Consists of one or more dependent clauses plus two or more independent clauses.
> *When Mother asked the girls to demonstrate their newfound skills, Joyce wrote a letter, and Dot drew a picture.*

Note: Do **not** confuse compound sentence elements with compound sentences.

Simple sentences with compound subjects:
> *Joyce and Dot wrote letters.*
> *The girl in row three and the boy next to her were passing notes across the aisle.*

Simple sentences with compound predicates:
> Joyce _wrote letters_ and _drew pictures_.
> The captain of the high school debate team _graduated with honors_ and _studied broadcast journalism in college_.

Simple sentence with compound object of preposition:
> Coleen graded the students' essays for _style_ and _mechanical accuracy_.

Through critical analysis, you can recognize a piece of writing that is unified, coherent, and well developed. To achieve unity, the writer will ensure that all parts work together to develop the thesis. Even the smallest detail can serve a purpose, such as developing the mood or setting the appropriate tone. To achieve coherence, the writer will use a structure that focuses on the main idea. In some cases, a transitional word or sentence will clarify the relationship of the ideas. For example, the author uses "because" to indicate cause and effect. This approach is more subtle than a direct announcement that Point A caused Point B. To achieve complete development, the author will strive for balance, providing the reader with sufficient and appropriate detail.

Unity

Usually, prose that lacks unity fails for one of the following reasons: (1) it lacks a clear statement of a main idea; (2) the opening statement misdirects the reader because it makes a commitment that the writing does not—perhaps cannot—meet; (3) subdivisions are not so selected or phrased that they clarify their relation to the main idea.

A good topic statement works for the writer because it appropriately directs the writer's commitment. A topic sentence is only effective if the details that follow develop it and firm it up.

- The details may cite particulars, instances, examples, and illustrations. Probably the easiest way to clarify a topic sentence is to provide instances.
- On the other hand, an incident or extended illustration can also be used effectively. The writer may establish the topic sentence by telling a story or describing a single illustration in some detail. This extended illustration might be an analogy.
- Yet another way to develop a topic sentence is by using cause-and-effect speculations.
- Comparison and contrast are often used very effectively in establishing a point. It is like this, but not like that.
- Not used as often, but still a viable alternative, is a restatement and amplification of the topic sentence itself.

Focus

Point of view defines the focus a writer assumes in relation to a given topic. It is extremely important to maintain a consistent point of view in order to create coherent paragraphs. Point of view is related to matters of person, tense, tone, and number.

Person—A shift in the form that indicates whether a person is speaking (first), is being spoken to (second), or is being spoken about (third) can disrupt continuity of a passage. In your essay, it is recommended that you write in the third person, as it is often considered the most formal of the modes of person. If you do decide to use the more informal first or second person (I, you, or we) in your essay, be careful not to shift between first, second, and third persons from sentence to sentence or paragraph to paragraph.

Tense—Verb tenses indicate the time of an action or state of being—the past, present, or future. It is important to stick largely to a selected tense, though this may not always be the case. For instance, in an essay about the history of environmental protection, it might be necessary to include a paragraph about the future benefits or consequences of protecting the earth.

Tone—The tone of an essay varies greatly with the purpose, subject, and audience

Number—Words change when their meanings are singular or plural. Make sure that you do not shift number needlessly; if a meaning is singular in one sentence, do not make it plural in the subsequent sentence.

Techniques for revising written texts to achieve clarity and economy of expression

Enhancing Interest:

- Start out with an attention-grabbing introduction. This sets an engaging tone for the entire piece, and it will be more likely to pull in the reader.
- Use dynamic vocabulary and varied sentence beginnings. Keep the readers on their toes. If they can predict what you are going to say next, switch it up.
- Avoid using clichés (e.g., as cold as ice, the best thing since sliced bread, nip it in the bud). These are easy shortcuts, but they are not interesting, memorable, or convincing.

Ensuring Understanding:

- Avoid using the words, "clearly," "obviously," and "undoubtedly." Often, things that are clear or obvious to the author are not as apparent to the reader. Instead of using these words, make your point so strongly that it is clear on its own.
- Use the word that best fits the meaning you intend, even if it is longer or a little less common. Try to find a balance, and go with a familiar yet precise word.
- When in doubt, explain further.

The **organization** of a written work includes two factors: the order in which the writer has chosen to present the different parts of the discussion or argument and the relationships he or she constructs between these parts.

Written ideas need to be presented in a **logical order** so that a reader can follow the information easily and quickly. There are many different ways in which to order a series of ideas, but they all share one thing—to lead the reader along a desired path, while avoiding backtracking and skipping around, in order to give a clear, strong presentation of the writer's main idea. The following are *some* of the ways in which a paragraph may be organized.

Sequence of events—In this type of organization, the details are presented in the order in which they have occurred. Paragraphs that describe a process or procedure, give directions, or outline a given period (such as a day or a month) are often arranged chronologically.

Statement support—In this type of organization, the main idea is stated, and the rest of the paragraph explains or proves it. This is also referred to as relative or order of importance. This type of order is organized in four ways: most to least, least to most, most least most, and least most least.

Comparison-Contrast—The compare-contrast pattern is used when a paragraph describes the differences or similarities of two or more ideas, actions, events, or things. Usually, the topic sentence describes the basic relationship between the ideas or items, and the rest of the paragraph explains this relationship.

Classification—In this type of organization, the paragraph presents grouped information about a topic. The topic sentence usually states the general category, and the rest of the sentences show how various elements of the category have a common base and how they differ from the common base.

Cause-and-Effect—This pattern describes how two or more events are connected. The main sentence usually states the primary cause(s) and the primary effect(s), and their basic connection. The rest of the sentences explain the connection—how one event caused the next.

Spatial/Place—In this type of organization, certain descriptions are organized according to the location of items in relation to each other and to a larger context. The orderly arrangement guides the reader's eye as he or she mentally envisions the scene or place being described.

Example, Clarification, and Definition—These types of organizations show, explain, or elaborate on the main idea. This can be done by showing specific cases, examining meaning multiple times, or describing one term extensively.

Paragraphs should contain concrete, interesting information and supporting details to support the main idea or point of view. Fact statements add weight to opinions, especially when the writer is trying to convince the reader of his or her viewpoint. Because every good thesis has an assertion, a well-written passage offers specifics, facts, data, anecdotes, expert opinion, and other details to *show* or *prove* that assertion. While *the author* knows what he or she wants to convey, the *reader* does not.

Like a whole piece of writing, the paragraphs that make up that piece can take a number of forms or combinations of forms. These forms help create an organized and well-structured document:

Cause-and-effect is used to show the reasons for the result of some action.

Compare-and-contrast is used to show similarities and differences between two or more items.

Definition is used if a simple dictionary definition is not sufficient.

Example and illustration is used to show a point by citing examples.

Sequence and process is used to show a step-by-step procedure.

A piece of writing should end with a brief straightforward **concluding paragraph** that ties together the written content and leaves the reader with a sense of its completion. The conclusion should reinforce the main points and offer some insight into the topic, provide a sense of unity for the essay by relating it to the thesis, and signal clear closure of the essay.

Techniques for revising written texts to achieve clarity and economy of expression

Enhancing Interest:

- Start out with an attention-grabbing introduction. This sets an engaging tone for the entire piece, and it will be more likely to pull in the reader.
- Use dynamic vocabulary and varied sentence beginnings. Keep the readers on their toes. If they can predict what you are going to say next, switch it up.
- Avoid using clichés (e.g., as cold as ice, the best thing since sliced bread, nip it in the bud). These are easy shortcuts, but they are not interesting, memorable, or convincing.

Ensuring Understanding:

- Avoid using the words, "clearly," "obviously," and "undoubtedly." Often, things that are clear or obvious to the author are not as apparent to the reader. Instead of using these words, make your point so strongly that it is clear on its own.
- Use the word that best fits the meaning you intend, even if it is longer or a little less common. Try to find a balance, and go with a familiar yet precise word.
- When in doubt, explain further.

Revision of sentences to eliminate wordiness, ambiguity, and redundancy

Sometimes students see this exercise as simply catching errors in spelling or word use. Students need to reframe their thinking about revising and editing. Some questions that need to be asked include:
- Is the reasoning coherent?
- Is the point established?
- Does the introduction make the reader want to read this discourse?
- What is the thesis? Is it proven?
- What is the purpose? Is it clear? Is it useful, valuable, and interesting?
- Is the style of writing so wordy that it exhausts the reader and interferes with engagement?
- Is the writing so spare that it is boring?
- Are the sentences too uniform in structure?
- Are there too many simple sentences?
- Are too many of the complex sentences the same structure?
- Are the compounds truly compounds, or are they unbalanced?
- Are parallel structures truly parallel?
- If there are characters, are they believable?
- If there is dialogue, is it natural or stilted?

- Is the title appropriate?
- Does the writing show creativity, or is it boring?
- Is the language appropriate? Is it too formal? Too informal? If jargon is used, is it appropriate?

Studies have clearly demonstrated that the most fertile area in teaching writing is this one. If students can learn to revise their own work effectively, they are well on their way to becoming effective, mature writers. Word processing is an important tool for teaching this stage in the writing process. Microsoft Word has tracking features that make the revision exchanges between teachers and students more effective than ever before.

Techniques to Maintain Focus

- **Focus on a main point.** The point should be clear to readers, and all sentences in the paragraph should relate to it.
- **Start the paragraph with a topic sentence.** This should be a general, one-sentence summary of the paragraph's main point, relating both back towards the thesis and toward the content of the paragraph. (A topic sentence is sometimes unnecessary if the paragraph continues a developing idea clearly introduced in a preceding paragraph, or if the paragraph appears in a narrative of events, where generalizations might interrupt the flow of the story.)
- **Stick to the point.** Eliminate sentences that do not support the topic sentence.
- **Be flexible.** If there is not enough evidence to support the claim your topic sentence is making, do not fall into the trap of wandering or introducing new ideas within the paragraph. Either find more evidence, or adjust the topic sentence to collaborate with the available evidence.

Here's a piece of writing that exemplifies these principles. Notice how the essay writer identifies the ways that the structure of the writing helps to develop the theme.

Sample Prompt and Well-Written Response:

Written on July 15, 1944, three weeks before the Nazis arrested the Frank family, Anne's diary entry explains her worldview and future hopes.

> *It's difficult in times like these: ideals, dreams, and cherished hopes rise within us, only to be crushed by grim reality. It's a wonder I haven't abandoned all my ideals; they seem so absurd and impractical. Yet I cling to them because I still believe, in spite of everything, that people are truly good at heart.*

> *It's utterly impossible for me to build my life on a foundation of chaos, suffering, and death. I see the world being slowly transformed into a wilderness, I hear the approaching thunder that, one day, will destroy us too, I feel the suffering of millions, and yet, when I look up at the sky, I somehow feel that everything will change for the better, that this cruelty too shall end, that peace and tranquility will return once more. In the meantime, I must hold on to my ideals. Perhaps the day will come when I will be able to realize them!*

Using your knowledge of literature, write a response in which you:

- Compare and contrast Anne's ideals with her awareness of the conditions in which she lives; and
- Discuss how the structure of Anne's writing—her sentences and paragraphs—emphasize the above contrast.

This excerpt from The Diary of Anne Frank reveals the inner strength of a young girl who refuses, despite the wartime violence and danger surrounding her, to let her idealism be overcome by hatred and mass killing. This idealism is reflected, in part, by her emphases on universal human hopes, such as peace, tranquility, and goodwill. However, Anne Frank is no dreamy Pollyanna. Reflecting on her idealism in the context of the war raging around her, she matter-of-factly writes, "My dreams, they seem so absurd and impractical."

This indicates Anne Frank's awareness of not only her own predicament, but of human miseries that extend beyond the immediate circumstances of her life. For elsewhere, she writes in a similar vein, "In times like these… I see the world being slowly transformed into a wilderness"; despite her own suffering, she can "feel the suffering of millions."

Yet Anne Frank believes, "in spite of everything, that people are truly good at heart." This statement epitomizes the stark existential contrast of her worldview with the wartime reality that ultimately claimed her life.

The statement also exemplifies how Anne's literary form—her syntax and diction—mirror thematic content and contrasts. "In spite of everything," she still believes in people. She can "hear the approaching thunder…yet, when I look up at the sky, I somehow feel that everything will change for the better." At numerous points in this diary entry, first-hand knowledge of violent tragedy stands side-by-side with belief in humanity and human progress.

"I must hold on to my ideals," Anne concludes. "Perhaps the day will come when I'll be able to realize them!" In her diary, she has done so, and more.

0012   Understand how to promote students' knowledge of correct spelling, usage, and other writing mechanics.

A verb must correspond in the singular or plural form with the simple subject; it is not affected by any interfering elements. Note: A simple subject is never found in a prepositional phrase (a phrase beginning with a word such as of, by, over, through, until).

Present Tense Verb Form

	Singular	Plural
1st person (talking about oneself)	I do	We do
2nd person (talking to another)	You do	You do
3rd person (talking about someone or something)	He She does It	They do

Error: Sally, as well as her sister, plan to go into nursing.

Problem: The subject in the sentence is *Sally* alone, not the word *sister*. Therefore, the verb must be singular.

Correction: *Sally, as well as her sister, plans to go into nursing.*

Error: There has been many car accidents lately on that street.

Problem: The subject *accidents* in this sentence is plural; the verb must be plural also—even though it comes before the subject.

Correction: *There have been many car accidents lately on that street.*

Error: Everyone of us have a reason to attend the school musical.

Problem: The simple subject is *everyone*, not the *us* in the prepositional phrase. Therefore, the verb must be singular also.

Correction: *Everyone of us has a reason to attend the school musical.*

Error: Either the police captain or his officers is going to the convention.

Problem: In either/or and neither/nor constructions, the verb agrees with the subject closer to it.

Correction: *Either the police captain or his officers are going to the convention.*

PRACTICE EXERCISE—SUBJECT-VERB AGREEMENT

Choose the option that corrects an error in the underlined portion(s).
If no error exists, choose "No change is necessary."

1)   Every year, the store <u>stays</u> open late, when shoppers desperately <u>try</u> to purchase Christmas presents as they <u>prepare</u> for the holiday.

    A. stay
    B. tries
    C. prepared
    D. No change is necessary.

2)   Paul McCartney, together with George Harrison and Ringo Starr, <u>sing</u> classic Beatles songs on a special greatest-hits CD.

    A. singing
    B. sings
    C. sung
    D. No change is necessary.

3)   My friend's cocker spaniel, while <u>chasing</u> cats across the street, always <u>manages</u> to <u>knock</u> over the trash cans.

    A. chased
    B. manage
    C. knocks
    D. No change is necessary.

4)   Some of the ice on the driveway <u>have melted.</u>

   A. having melted
   B. has melted
   C. has melt.
   D. No change is necessary.

5)   Neither the criminal forensics expert nor the DNA blood evidence
     <u>provide</u> enough support for that verdict.

   A. provides
   B. were providing
   C. are providing
   D. No change is necessary.

ANSWER KEY: PRACTICE EXERCISE FOR SUBJECT-VERB AGREEMENT

1) D   Option D is correct because *store* is third-person singular and
            requires the third-person singular verbs *stays*. Option B is
            incorrect because the plural noun *shoppers* requires a plural
            verb *try*. In Option C, there is no reason to shift to the past tense
            prepared.

2) B   Option B is correct because the subject, *Paul McCartney,*
            is singular and requires the singular verb *sings*. Option A is
            incorrect because the present participle *singing* does not
            stand alone as a verb. Option C is incorrect because the past
            participle *sung* alone cannot function as the verb in this sentence.

3) D   Option D is the correct answer because the subject *cocker spaniel*
            is singular and requires the singular verb *manages*. Options A, B,
            and C do not work structurally with the sentence.

4) B   The subject of the sentence is *some*, which requires a third-person
            singular verb *has melted.* Option A incorrectly uses the present
            participle *having*, which does not act as a helping verb. Option C
            does not work structurally with the sentence.

5) A   In Option A, the singular subject *evidence* is closer to the verb
            and thus requires the singular in the neither/nor construction.
            Both Options B and C are plural forms with the helping verb and
            the present participle.

Past tense and past participles

Both regular and irregular verbs must appear in their standard forms for each tense. Note: the -ed or -d ending is added to regular verbs in the past tense and for past participles.

Infinitive	Past Tense	Past Participle
Bake	Baked	Baked

Irregular Verb Forms

Infinitive	Past Tense	Past Participle
Be	Was, were	Been
Become	Became	Become
Break	Broke	Broken
Bring	Brought	Brought
Choose	Chose	Chosen
Come	Came	Come
Do	Did	Done
Draw	Drew	Drawn
Eat	Ate	Eaten
Fall	Fell	Fallen
Forget	Forgot	Forgotten
Freeze	Froze	Frozen
Give	Gave	Given
Go	Went	Gone
Grow	Grew	Grown
Have/has	Had	Had
Hide	Hid	Hidden
Know	Knew	Known
Lay	Laid	Laid
Lie	Lay	Lain
Ride	Rode	Ridden
Rise	Rose	Risen
Run	Ran	Run
See	Saw	Seen
Steal	Stole	Stolen
Take	Took	Taken
Tell	Told	Told
Throw	Threw	Thrown
Wear	Wore	Worn
Write	Wrote	Written

Error: She should have went to her doctor's appointment at the scheduled time.

Problem: The past participle of the verb *to go* is *gone*. *Went* expresses the simple past tense.

Correction: *She should have gone to her doctor's appointment at the scheduled time.*

Error: My train is suppose to arrive before two o'clock.

Problem: The verb following *train* is a present tense passive construction, which requires the present tense verb *to be* and the past participle.

Correction: *My train is supposed to arrive before two o'clock.*

Error: Linda should of known that the car wouldn't start after leaving it out in the cold all night.

Problem: *Should of* is a nonstandard expression. *Of* is not a verb.

Correction: *Linda should have known that the car wouldn't start after leaving it out in the cold all night.*

PRACTICE EXERCISE—STANDARD VERB FORMS

Choose the option that corrects an error in the underlined portion(s). If no error exists, choose "No change is necessary."

1)   My professor had knew all along that we would pass his course.

   A. know
   B. had known
   C. knowing
   D. No change is necessary

2)   Kevin was asked to erase the vulgar words he had wrote.

   A. writes
   B. has write
   C. had written
   D. No change is necessary

3)   Melanie <u>had forget</u> to tell her parents that she left the cat in the closet.

      A. had forgotten
      B. forgot
      C. forget
      D. No change is necessary

4)   Craig always <u>leave</u> the house a mess when his parents are not there.

      A. left
      B. leaves
      C. leaving
      D. No change is necessary

5)   The store manager accused Kathy of <u>having stole</u> more than five hundred dollars from the safe.

      A. has stolen
      B. having stolen
      C. stole
      D. No change is necessary

ANSWER KEY: PRACTICE EXERCISE FOR STANDARD VERB FORMS

1. B   Option B is correct because the past participle needs the helping verb *had*. Option A is incorrect because *it* is in the infinitive tense. Option C incorrectly uses the present participle.

2. C   Option C is correct because the past participle follows the helping verb *had*. Option A uses the verb in the present tense. Option B is an incorrect use of the verb.

3. A   Option A is correct because the past participle uses the helping verb *had*. Option B uses the wrong form of the verb. Option C uses the wrong form of the verb.

4. B   Option B correctly uses the past tense of the verb. Option A uses the verb in an incorrect way. Option C uses the verb without a helping verb such as *is*.

5. B   Option B is correct because it is the past participle. Option A and C use the verb incorrectly.

Inappropriate shifts in verb tense

Verb tenses must refer to the same time consistently, unless a change in time is required.

Error: Despite the increased number of students in the school this year, overall attendance is higher last year at the sporting events.

Problem: The verb *is* represents an inconsistent shift to the present tense when the action refers to a past occurrence.

Correction: *Despite the increased number of students in the school this year, overall attendance was higher last year at sporting events.*

Error: My friend Lou, who just competed in the marathon, ran since he was twelve years old.

Problem: Because Lou continues to run, the present perfect tense is needed.

Correction: *My friend Lou, who just competed in the marathon, has run since he was twelve years old.*

Error: The Mayor congratulated Wallace Mangham, who renovates the city hall last year.

Problem: Although the speaker is talking in the present, the action of renovating the city hall was in the past.

Correction: *The Mayor congratulated Wallace Mangham, who renovated the city hall last year.*

PRACTICE EXERCISE—SHIFTS IN TENSE

Choose the option that corrects an error in the underlined portion(s). If no error exists, choose "No change is necessary."

1)   After we <u>washed</u> the fruit that had <u>growing</u> in the garden, we knew there <u>was</u> a store that would buy them.

   A) washing
   B) grown
   C) is
   D) No change is necessary.

2)   The tourists <u>used</u> to visit the Atlantic City boardwalk whenever they
      <u>vacationed</u> during the summer. Unfortunately, their numbers have
      <u>diminished</u> every year.

   A) use
   B) vacation
   C) diminish
   D) No change is necessary.

3)   When the temperature <u>drops</u> to below thirty-two degrees Fahrenheit,
      the water on the lake<u> freezes</u>, which <u>allowed</u> children to skate across it.

   A) dropped
   B) froze
   C) allows
   D) No change is necessary.

4)   The artists were <u>hired</u> to <u>create</u> a monument that would pay tribute to
      the men who were <u>killed</u> in World War II.

   A) hiring
   B) created
   C) killing
   D) No change is necessary.

5)   Emergency medical personnel rushed to the scene of the shooting,
      where many injured people <u>waiting</u> for treatment.
   A) wait
   B) waited
   C) waits
   D) No change is necessary.

ANSWER KEY: PRACTICE EXERCISE FOR SHIFTS IN TENSE

1) B   The past participle *grown* is needed instead of *growing,* which
        is the progressive tense. Option A is incorrect because
        the past participle *washed* takes the *-ed*. Option C incorrectly
        replaces the past participle *was* with the present tense *is*.

2) D   Option A is incorrect because *use* is the present tense. Option
        B incorrectly uses the noun *vacation*. Option C incorrectly uses
        the present tense *diminish* instead of the past tense *diminished*.

3) C   The present tense *allows* is necessary in the context of the
        sentence. Option A is incorrect because *dropped* is a past
        participle. Option B is incorrect because *froze* is also a
        past participle.

4) D   Option A is incorrect because *hiring* is the present tense.
                  Option B is incorrect because *created* is a past participle.
                  In Option C, *killing* does not fit into the context of the sentence.

5) B   In Option B, *waited* corresponds with the past tense *rushed*.
                  In Option A, *wait* is incorrect because it is present tense.
                  In Option C, *waits* is incorrect because the noun *people*
                  is plural and requires the singular form of the verb.

Agreements between pronoun and antecedent

A pronoun must correspond to its antecedent in number (singular or plural), person (first, second, or third person) and gender (male, female, or neutral). A pronoun must refer clearly to a single word, not to a complete idea.

A **pronoun shift** is a grammatical error in which the author starts a sentence, paragraph, or section of a paper using one particular type of pronoun and then suddenly shifts to another. This often confuses the reader.

Error: A teacher should treat all their students fairly.

Problem: Since *teacher* is singular, the pronoun referring to it must also be singular. Otherwise, the noun has to be made plural.

Correction: *Teachers should treat all their students fairly.*

Error: When an actor is rehearsing for a play, it often helps if you can memorize the lines in advance.

Problem: *Actor* is a third-person word; that is, the writer is talking about the subject. The pronoun *you* is in the second person, which means the writer is talking to the subject.

Correction: *When actors are rehearsing for plays, it helps if they can memorize the lines in advance.*

Error: The workers in the factory were upset when his or her paychecks did not arrive on time.

Problem: *Workers* is a plural form, while *his or her* refers to one person.

Correction: *The workers in the factory were upset when their paychecks did not arrive on time.*

Error: The charity auction was highly successful, which pleased everyone.

Problem: In this sentence, the pronoun *which* refers to the idea of the auction's success. In fact, *which* has no antecedent in the sentence; the word *success* is not stated.

Correction: *Everyone was pleased at the success of the auction.*

Error: Lana told Melanie that she would like aerobics.

Problem: The person that *she* refers to is unclear; it could be either Lana or Melanie.

Correction: *Lana said that Melanie would like aerobics.*

-OR-

Lana told Melanie that she, Melanie, would like aerobics.

Error: I dislike accounting, even though my brother is one.

Problem: A person's occupation is not the same as a field, and the pronoun *one* is thus incorrect. Note that the word *accountant* is not used in the sentence, so *one* has no antecedent.

Correction: *I dislike accounting, even though my brother is an accountant.*

PRACTICE EXERCISE—PRONOUN/ANTECEDENT AGREEMENT

Choose the option that corrects an error in the underlined portion(s).
If no error exists, choose "No change is necessary."

1) <u>You</u> can get to Martha's Vineyard by driving from Boston to Woods Hole. Once there, you can travel over on a ship, but <u>you</u> may find traveling by <u>airplane</u> to be an exciting experience.

   A. They
   B. visitors
   C. it
   D. No change is necessary.

2) Both the city leader and the <u>journalist</u> are worried about the new interstate; <u>she fears</u> <u>the new roadway</u> will destroy precious farmland.

   A. journalist herself
   B. they fear
   C. it
   D. No change is necessary.

3) When <u>hunters</u> are looking for deer in <u>the woods</u>, <u>you</u> must remain quiet for long periods.

    A. they
    B. it
    C. we
    D. No change is necessary.

4) Florida's strong economy is based on the importance of the citrus industry. <u>Producing</u> orange juice for most of the country.

    A. They produce
    B. Who produce
    C. Farmers there produce
    D. No change is necessary.

5) Dr. Kennedy told Paul Elliot, <u>his</u> assistant, that <u>he</u> would have to finish grading the tests before going home, no matter how long <u>it</u> took.

    A. their
    B. he, Paul
    C. they
    D. No change is necessary.

ANSWER KEY: PRACTICE EXERCISE FOR PRONOUN AGREEMENT

1) D   Pronouns must be consistent. As *you* is used throughout the sentence, the shift to *visitors* is incorrect. Option A, *They*, is vague and unclear. Option C, *it*, is also unclear.

2) B   The plural pronoun *they* is necessary to agree with the two nouns *leader* and *journalist*. There is no need for the reflexive pronoun *herself* in Option A. Option C, *it*, is vague.

3) A   The shift to *you* is unnecessary. The plural pronoun *they* is necessary to agree with the noun *hunters*. The word *we* in Option C is vague; the reader does not know to whom the word *we* might refer. Option B, *it*, has no antecedent.

4) C   The noun *farmers* is needed for clarification because *producing* is vague. Option A is incorrect because *they produce* is vague. Option B is incorrect because *who* has no antecedent and creates a fragment.

5) B   The repetition of the name *Paul* is necessary to clarify to whom the pronoun *he* is referring. (It could be Dr. Kennedy.) Option A is incorrect because the singular pronoun *his* is needed, not the plural pronoun *their*. Option C is incorrect because the pronoun *it* refers to the plural noun *tests*.

Rules for clear pronoun references:

Make sure that the antecedent reference is clear and cannot refer to something else.

A "distant relative" is a relative pronoun or a relative clause that has been placed too far away from the antecedent to which it refers. It is a common error to place a verb between the relative pronoun and its antecedent.

Error: Return the books to the library that are overdue.
Problem: The relative clause "that are overdue" refers to the "books" and should be placed immediately after the antecedent.
Correction: Return the books that are overdue to the library.
-or-
Return the overdue books to the library.

A pronoun should not refer to adjectives or possessive nouns.

Adjectives, nouns, or possessive pronouns should not be used as antecedents. This will create ambiguity in sentences.

Error: In Todd's letter, he told his mom he'd broken the priceless vase.

Problem: In this sentence, the pronoun "he" seems to refer to the noun phrase "Todd's letter," though it was probably meant to refer to the possessive noun "Todd's."

Correction: In his letter, Todd told his mom that he had broken the priceless vase.

A pronoun should not refer to an implied idea.

A pronoun must refer to a specific antecedent rather than an implied antecedent. When an antecedent is not stated specifically, the reader has to guess or assume the meaning of a sentence. Pronouns that do not have antecedents are called expletives. "It" and "there" are the most common expletives, though other pronouns can also become expletives as well. In informal conversation, expletives allow for casual presentation of ideas without supporting evidence; however, in writing that is more formal, it is best to be more precise.

Error: She said that it is important to floss every day.

Problem: The pronoun "it" refers to an implied idea.

Correction: She said that flossing every day is important.

Error: They returned the book because there were missing pages.

Problem: The pronouns "they" and "there" do not refer to the antecedent.

Correction: The customer returned the book with missing pages.

Using Who, That, and Which

Who, whom and **whose** refer to human beings and can either introduce essential or nonessential clauses. **That** refers to things other than humans and it is used to introduce essential clauses. **Which** refers to things other than humans and it is used to introduce nonessential clauses.

Error: The doctor that performed the surgery said the man would be fully recovered.

Problem: Since the relative pronoun is referring to a human, who should be used.

Correction: The doctor who performed the surgery said the man would be fully recovered.

Error: That ice cream cone that you just ate looked delicious.

Problem: That has already been used so you must use *which* to introduce the next clause, whether it is essential or nonessential.

Correction: That ice cream cone, which you just ate, looked delicious.

Proper case forms

Pronouns, unlike nouns, change case forms. Pronouns must be in the subjective, objective, or possessive form according to their functions in the sentence.

Personal Pronouns

Subjective (Nominative)		Possessive		Objective	
Singular	Plural	Singular	Plural	Singular	Plural
1st person — I	We	My	Our	Me	Us
2nd person — You	You	Your	Your	You	You
3rd person — He She It	They	His Her Its	Their	Him Her It	Them

Relative Pronouns

Who   Subjective/Nominative
Whom   Objective
Whose   Possessive

Error: Tom and me have reserved seats for next week's baseball game.

Problem: The pronoun *me* is the subject of the verb *have reserved* and should be in the subjective form.

Correction: *Tom and I have reserved seats for next week's baseball game.*

Error: Mr. Green showed all of we students how to make paper hats.

Problem: The pronoun *we* is the object of the preposition *of*. It should be in the objective form, *us*.

Correction: *Mr. Green showed all of us students how to make paper hats.*

Error: Who's coat is this?

Problem: The interrogative possessive pronoun is *whose*; *who's* is the contraction for who is.

Correction: *Whose coat is this?*

Error: The voters will choose the candidate whom has the best qualifications for the job.

Problem: The case of the relative pronoun *who* or *whom* is determined by the pronoun's function in the clause in which it appears. The word who is in the subjective case, and whom is in the objective. Analyze how the pronoun is being used within the sentence.

Correction: *The voters will choose the candidate who has the best qualifications for the job.*

PRACTICE EXERCISE—PRONOUN CASE

Choose the option that corrects an error in the underlined portion(s). If no error exists, choose "No change is necessary."

1) Even though Sheila and <u>he</u> had planned to be alone at the diner, <u>they</u> were joined by three friends of <u>their's</u> instead.

    A) him
    B) him and her
    C) theirs
    D) No change is necessary.

2) Uncle Walter promised to give his car to <u>whomever</u> will guarantee to drive it safely.

    A) whom
    B) whoever
    C) them
    D) No change is necessary.

3) Eddie and <u>him</u> gently laid <u>the body</u> on the ground next to <u>the sign</u>.

    A) he
    B) them
    C) it
    D) No change is necessary.

4) Mary, <u>who</u> is competing in the chess tournament, is a better player than <u>me</u>.

    A) whose
    B) whom
    C) I
    D) No change is necessary.

5) <u>We, ourselves</u>, have decided not to buy property in that development; however, our friends have already bought <u>themselves</u> some land.

    A) We, ourself,
    B) their selves
    C) their self
    D) No change is necessary.

ANSWER KEY: PRACTICE EXERCISE FOR PRONOUN CASE

1) C   The possessive pronoun *theirs* does not need an apostrophe. Option A is incorrect because the subjective pronoun *he* is needed in this sentence. Option B is incorrect because the subjective pronoun *they*, not the objective pronouns *him* and *her*, is needed.

2) B   The subjective case *whoever*—not the objective case *whomever*—is the subject of the relative clause *whoever will guarantee to drive it safely*. Option A is incorrect because *whom* is an objective pronoun. Option C is incorrect because *car* is singular and takes the pronoun *it*.

3) A   The subjective pronoun *he* is needed as the subject of the verb *laid*. Option B is incorrect because *them* is vague; the noun *body* is needed to clarify *it*. Option C is incorrect because *it* is vague, and the noun *sign* is necessary for clarification.

4) C   The subjective pronoun *I* is needed because the comparison is understood. Option A incorrectly uses the possessive *whose*. Option B is incorrect because the subjective pronoun *who*, and not the objective *whom*, is needed.

5) D   The reflexive pronoun *themselves* refers to the plural *friends*. Option A is incorrect because the plural *we* requires the reflexive *ourselves*. Option C is incorrect because the possessive pronoun *their* is never joined with either *self* or *selves*.

Demonstrative pronouns

The four demonstrative pronouns are **this, that, these, and those**.

This and *these* refer to something nearby in time and space.
That and *those* refer to something farther away in time and space.

This and *that* are singular.
These and *those* are plural.

These words can also be used as adjectives.

Examples:

This is an exciting book.
This is a singular pronoun and refers to the book, which is near the speaker.

This book is exciting.
This is a singular adjective and modifies *book,* which is near the speaker.

That is a classic-looking car.
That is a singular pronoun and refers to the car, which is away from the speaker.

That car is classic looking.
That is a singular adjective and modifies *car,* which is away from the speaker.

These are very interesting antiques.
These is a plural pronoun and refers to antiques, which are near the speaker.

These antiques are interesting.
These is a plural adjective and modifies the word *antiques*, which are near the speaker.

We bought those at the antique fair.
Those is a plural pronoun and refers to whatever was bought at the fair.

We bought those chairs at the antique fair.
Those is a plural adjective and modifies *chairs*, which are away from the speaker.

Commas

Commas indicate a brief pause. They are used to set off dependent clauses and long introductory word groups, to separate words in a series, to set off unimportant material that interrupts the flow of the sentence, and to separate independent clauses joined by conjunctions.

Error: After I finish my master's thesis I plan to work in Chicago.

Problem: A comma is needed after an introductory dependent word group containing a subject and verb.

Correction: *After I finish my master's thesis, I plan to work in Chicago.*

Error: I washed waxed and vacuumed my car today.

Problem: Commas should separate nouns, phrases, or clauses in a list, as well as two or more coordinate adjectives that modify one word. Although the word *and* is sometimes considered optional, it is often necessary to clarify the meaning.

Correction: *I washed, waxed, and vacuumed my car today.*

Error: She was a talented dancer but she is mostly remembered for her singing ability.

Problem: A comma is needed before a conjunction that joins two independent clauses (complete sentences).

Correction: *She was a talented dancer, but she is mostly remembered for her singing ability.*

Periods

Periods are used as end marks to declarative and imperative sentences. A declarative sentence makes a statement. An imperative sentence makes a request or issues a command.

- Declarative sentence: Now is the winter of our discontent.
- Imperative sentence: Please sign your name to this contract.

Periods are used in other cases as well:

- An indirect question: She wondered when the train would come.
- In abbreviations: Dr. White arrived in Washington, D.C., at 10: a.m.
- As decimal points: With tax, my lunch was $10.85.

Exclamation Points
Use exclamation points to express strong feeling, emotion, or urgency.

- Wow, what a day!
- I hate spinach!
- Hurry or we'll miss the bus!

To show especially strong feeling, writers may want to use more than one exclamation point. Generally, three are sufficient!!! But this type of strong expression is not used in formal writing.

Semicolons and colons

Semicolons are needed to separate two or more closely related independent clauses when the second clause is introduced by a transitional adverb. (These clauses may also be written as separate sentences, preferably by placing the adverb within the second sentence). **Colons** are used to introduce lists and to emphasize what follows.

Error: I climbed to the top of the mountain, it took me three hours.

Problem: A comma alone cannot separate two independent clauses. Instead, a semicolon is needed to separate two related sentences.

Correction: *I climbed to the top of the mountain; it took me three hours.*

Error: In the movie, asteroids destroyed Dallas, Texas, Kansas City, Missouri, and Boston, Massachusetts.

Problem: Semicolons are needed to separate items in a series that already contain internal punctuation.

Correction: *In the movie, asteroids destroyed Dallas, Texas; Kansas City, Missouri; and Boston, Massachusetts.*

Error: Essays will receive the following grades, A for excellent, B for good, C for average, and D for unsatisfactory.

Problem: A colon is needed to emphasize the information or list that follows.

Correction: *Essays will receive the following grades: A for excellent, B for good, C for average, and D for unsatisfactory.*

Error: The school carnival included: amusement rides, clowns, food booths, and a variety of games.

Problem: The material preceding the colon and the list that follows is not a complete sentence. Do not separate a verb (or preposition) from the object.

Correction: *The school carnival included amusement rides, clowns, food booths, and a variety of games.*

Apostrophes

Apostrophes are used to show either contractions or possession.

Error: She shouldnt be permitted to smoke cigarettes in the building.

Problem: An apostrophe is needed in a contraction in place of the missing letter.

Correction: *She shouldn't be permitted to smoke cigarettes in the building.*

Error: My cousins motorcycle was stolen from his driveway.

Problem: An apostrophe is needed to show possession.

Correction: *My cousin's motorcycle was stolen from his driveway.*
(Note: The use of the apostrophe before the letter "s" means that there is just one cousin. The plural form would read the following way: My cousins' motorcycle was stolen from their driveway.)

Error: The childrens new kindergarten teacher was also a singer.

Problem: An apostrophe is needed to show possession.

Correction: *The children's' new kindergarten teacher was also a singer.*

Error: Children screams could be heard for miles.

Problem: An apostrophe and the letter *s* are needed in the sentence to show whose screams they are.

Correction: *Children's screams could be heard for miles.*
(Note: Because the word children is already plural, the apostrophe and *s* must be added afterward to show ownership.)

Quotation marks

In a quoted statement that is either declarative or imperative, place the period inside the closing quotation marks.

> "The airplane crashed on the runway during takeoff."

If the quotation is followed by other words in the sentence, place a comma inside the closing quotations marks and a period at the end of the sentence.

> "The airplane crashed on the runway during takeoff," said the announcer.

In most instances in which a quoted title or expression occurs at the end of a sentence, the period is placed before either the single or double quotation marks.

"The middle school readers were unprepared to understand Bryant's poem 'Thanatopsis.'"

Early book-length adventure stories such as *Don Quixote* and *The Three Musketeers* were known as "picaresque novels."

The final quotation mark would precede the period if the content of the sentence were about a speech or quote so that the understanding of the meaning would be confused by the placement of the period.

The first thing out of his mouth was, "Hi, I'm home."
-but-
The first line of his speech began, "I arrived home to an empty house".

In sentences that are interrogatory or exclamatory, the question mark or exclamation point should be positioned outside the closing quotation marks if the quote itself is a statement or command or cited title.

Who decided to lead us in the recitation of the "Pledge of Allegiance"?

Why was Tillie shaking as she began her recitation, "Once upon a midnight dreary..."?

I was embarrassed when Mrs. White said, "Your slip is showing"!

In sentences that are declarative, but the quotation is a question or an exclamation, place the question mark or exclamation point inside the quotation marks.

The hall monitor yelled, "Fire! Fire!"

"Fire! Fire!" yelled the hall monitor.

Cory shrieked, "Is there a mouse in the room?" (In this instance, the question supersedes the exclamation.)

Quotations—whether words, phrases, or clauses—should be punctuated according to the rules of the grammatical function they serve in the sentence.

The works of Shakespeare, "the bard of Avon," have been contested as originating with other authors.

"You'll get my money," the old man warned, "when 'Hell freezes over'."

Sheila cited the passage that began "Four score and seven years ago...."
(Note the ellipsis followed by an enclosed period.)

"Old Ironsides" inspired the preservation of the U. S. S. Constitution.

Use quotation marks to enclose the titles of shorter works: songs, short
poems, short stories, essays, and chapters of books. (See "Using Italics" for
punctuating longer titles.)

"The Tell-Tale Heart"   "Casey at the Bat"   "America the Beautiful"

Dashes and Italics

Place **dashes** to denote sudden breaks in thought.

Some periods in literature—the Romantic Age, for example—
spanned different periods in different countries.

Use dashes instead of commas if commas are already used elsewhere in the
sentence for amplification or explanation.

The Fireside Poets included three Brahmans—James Russell
Lowell, Henry David Wadsworth, Oliver Wendell Holmes—
and John Greenleaf Whittier.

Use **italics** to punctuate the titles of long works of literature, names of
periodical publications, musical scores, works of art and motion picture
television, and radio programs. (When unable to write in italics, students
should be instructed to underline in their own writing where italics would
be appropriate.)

The Idylls of the King   *Hiawatha*   *The Sound and the Fury*
Mary Poppins   *Newsweek*   *The Nutcracker Suite*

Capitalize all proper names of persons (including specific organizations or
agencies of government); places (countries, states, cities, parks, and specific
geographical areas); and things (political parties, structures, historical and
cultural terms, and calendar and time designations); and religious terms (any
deity, revered person or group, sacred writings).

Percy Bysshe Shelley, Argentina, Mount Rainier National Park,
Grand Canyon, League of Nations, the Sears Tower, Birmingham,
Lyric Theater, Americans, Midwesterners, Democrats, Renaissance,
Boy Scouts of America, Easter, God, Bible, Dead Sea Scrolls, Koran

Capitalize proper adjectives and titles used with proper names.

California Gold Rush, President John Adams, French fries, Homeric epic, Romanesque architecture, Senator John Glenn

Note: Some words that represent titles and offices are not capitalized unless used with a proper name.

Capitalized	Not Capitalized
Congressman McKay	the congressman from Florida
Commander Alger	commander of the Pacific Fleet
Queen Elizabeth	the queen of England

Capitalize all main words in titles of works of literature, art, and music.

Error: Emma went to Dr. Peters for treatment since her own Doctor was on vacation.

Problem: The use of capital letters with Emma and Dr .Peters is correct since they are specific (proper) names; the title Dr. is also capitalized. However, the word *doctor* is not a specific name and should not be capitalized.

Correction: *Emma went to Dr. Peters for treatment since her own doctor was on vacation.*

Error: Our Winter Break does not start until next wednesday.

Problem: Days of the week are capitalized, but seasons are not capitalized.

Correction: *Our winter break does not start until next Wednesday.*

Error: The exchange student from israel, who came to study Biochemistry, spoke spanish very well.

Problem: Languages and the names of countries are always capitalized. Courses are also capitalized when they refer to a specific course; they are not capitalized when they refer to courses in general.

Correction: *The exchange student from Israel, who came to study Biochemistry, spoke Spanish very well.*

A good dictionary should replace the multiplicity and complexity of spelling rules based on phonics, letter doubling, and exceptions to rules not mastered by adulthood. As spelling mastery is also difficult for adolescents, our recommendation is the same. Learning the use of a dictionary and thesaurus will be a more rewarding use of time.

Most plurals of nouns that end in hard consonants or hard consonant sounds followed by a silent *e* are made by adding -*s*. Some words ending in vowels only add -*s*.

fingers, numerals, banks, bugs, riots, homes, gates, radios, bananas

Nouns that end in soft consonant sounds *s, j, x, z, ch,* and *sh,* add -*es*. Some nouns ending in *o* add -es.

dresses, waxes, churches, brushes, tomatoes

Nouns ending in *y* preceded by a vowel just add -*s*.

boys, alleys

Nouns ending in *y* preceded by a consonant change the *y* to *i* and add -*es*.

babies, corollaries, frugalities, poppies

Some nouns' plurals are formed irregularly or remain the same.

sheep, deer, children, leaves, oxen

Some nouns derived from foreign words, especially Latin, may make their plurals in two different ways—one of them Anglicized. Sometimes, the meanings are the same; other times, the two plurals are used in slightly different contexts. It is always wise to consult the dictionary.

appendices, appendixes   criterion, criteria
indexes, indices   crisis, crises

Make the plurals of closed (solid) compound words in the usual way except for words ending in –*ful,* which make their plurals on the root word.

timelines, hairpins

Make the plurals of open or hyphenated compounds by adding the change in inflection to the word that changes in number.

fathers-in-law, courts-martial, masters of art, doctors of medicine

Make the plurals of letters, numbers, and abbreviations by adding *-s.*

> fives and tens, IBMs, 1990s, *p*s and *q*s (Note that letters are italicized.)

Possessive nouns

Make the possessives of singular nouns by adding an apostrophe followed by the letter *s* (*'s*).

> baby's bottle, father's job, elephant's eye, teacher's desk, sympathizer's protests, week's postponement

Make the possessive of singular nouns ending in *s* by adding either an apostrophe or an (*'s*) depending upon common usage or sound. When making the possessive causes difficulty, use a prepositional phrase instead. Even with the sibilant ending, with a few exceptions, it is advisable to use the (*'s*) construction.

> dress's color, species' characteristics or characteristics of the species, James' hat or James's hat, Delores's shirt.

Make the possessive of plural nouns ending in *s* by adding the apostrophe after the *s.*
> horses' coats, jockeys' times, four days' time

Make possessives of plural nouns that do not end in *s* the same as singular nouns by adding *'s.*

> children's shoes, deer's antlers, cattle's horns

Make possessives of compound nouns by adding the inflection at the end of the word or phrase.

> the mayor of Los Angeles' campaign, the mailman's new truck, the mailmen's new trucks, my father-in-law's first wife, the keepsakes' values, several daughters-in-law's husbands

Note: Because a gerund functions as a noun, any noun preceding it and operating as a possessive adjective must reflect the necessary inflection. However, if the gerundive following the noun is a participle, no inflection is added.

> The general was perturbed by the private's sleeping on duty. (The word *sleeping* is a gerund, the object of the preposition *by.*
> -but-
> The general was perturbed to see the private sleeping on duty. (The word *sleeping* is a participle modifying *private.*)

0013   Understand writing and reading as tools for inquiry and research.

Although there may be times when teachers do not want students to read certain books texts, it is important to respect their choices when selecting reading material. Good readers often choose to read easy material simply because they do not want to be challenged. On the other hand, students who have difficulty in reading at grade level may be reluctant to read lower level books because it reinforces the knowledge that they cannot read as well as their peers. When they are unable to read material at grade level, it sets up a cycle of failure.

Teachers should try to have adequate reading material in the classroom library to meet the needs of the varying reading levels in the class. There should be a variety of reading material matching the themes and topics. By letting students know what their reading level is and pointing them in the right direction, it will help them experience success and therefore keep them reading.

The most important thing is that students are reading. Comic books in the classroom are perfectly acceptable as long as students are reading.

There are many ways teachers can encourage reading for pleasure in their classrooms. One of the best ways is to read aloud from a novel each day. Author studies in all grades will encourage students to seek out books by that author and read them on their own.

Even within the content areas, there is a wealth of fiction that relates to the theme at hand and provides students with background information that will help them with their studies. For example, when studying Colonial America in Social Studies, there are many illustrated books teachers can use as introductions for the lessons. Using part of the class to read aloud from a novel about that period in history will help students to develop an interest in reading about the themes and help them understand how much enjoyment reading can bring.

Monthly book clubs are also an excellent way of getting age-appropriate reading material into students' hands. Since these book clubs offer the books at fairly inexpensive prices, parents realize they can get more value for their money when they order each month. Book fairs at school provide students the chance to win books for themselves and their classrooms.

Throughout their lives, students will be reading a multitude of texts for a variety of purposes. The purpose behind reading often drives the type of reading completed by the student. The type of text can also drive the type of reading strategies the students use to successfully navigate the information.

When reading for pleasure, students tend to read less carefully, and may even skim some portions of the text. Because the book is simply for pleasure, this is perfectly acceptable and should be allowed. In fact, skimming skills can be introduced and used for other types of readings. Students who are looking for vocabulary words or definitions may skim a great deal of information at a more rapid pace before finding the appropriate part of the passage. This is also a good strategy when used to look for specific pieces of information.

In addition to skimming, scanning is another technique students can use to look through a large amount of text for specific details and/or information. This can be particularly helpful for students when they are searching through different books to determine if any of the information is pertinent to meet their needs.

Teachers need to take the time to teach students when it is necessary to reread information. Typically, students understand that it is important to reread when something is not understood clearly. However, there are other times when rereading may be important. In content-heavy texts, rereading can not only provide further clarification, it can also provide additional details the reader may have missed the first time. It is easy to miss information when so much is packed into small passages. Thus, rereading can be an important factor in learning and making sure students have absorbed all of the details.

In-depth reading can be a tiring task and difficult to complete on all books students encounter. Students need to understand that reading with an eye for detail is called for mostly in nonfiction texts which are laden with information. When reading in depth, students are trying to absorb as much information as possible.

Primary and secondary sources

The resources used to support a piece of writing can be divided into two major groups: primary sources and secondary sources.

Primary sources are works, records, etc. that were created during the period being studied or immediately after it. Secondary sources are works written significantly after the period being studied and are based upon primary sources. Primary sources are the basic materials that provide raw data and information. Secondary sources are the works that contain the explications of, and judgments on, this primary material.

Primary sources include the following kinds of materials:

- Documents that reflect the immediate, everyday concerns of people: memoranda, bills, deeds, charters, newspaper reports, pamphlets, graffiti, popular writings, journals or diaries, records of decision-making bodies, letters, receipts, snapshots, etc.

- Theoretical writings that reflect care and consideration in composition and an attempt to convince or persuade. The topic will generally be deeper and have more pervasive values than is the case with "immediate" documents. These may include newspaper or magazine editorials, sermons, political speeches, philosophical writings, etc.
- Narrative accounts of events, ideas, trends, etc., written with intentionality by someone contemporary with the events described
- Statistical data, although statistics may be misleading
- Literature and nonverbal materials, novels, stories, poetry, and essays from the period, as well as coins, archaeological artifacts, and art produced during the period

Secondary sources include the following kinds of materials:

- Books written based on primary materials about the period.
- Books written based on primary materials about persons who played a major role in the events under consideration.
- Books and articles written based on primary materials about the culture, the social norms, the language, and the values of the period.
- Quotations from primary sources
- Statistical data on the period
- The conclusions and inferences of other historians
- Multiple interpretations of the ethos of the time

The information a student, or for that matter a teacher, seeks can be located, if they understand where and how to locate it. Teaching students how to find, determine the appropriateness of, and utilize information gathered is an ongoing skill.

Teaching students to find information and select the most appropriate for the purpose can be a daunting task. The amount of information available today can seem overwhelming. Whittling it down into manageable chunks is essential for success.

In these cases, it can be helpful to coordinate services and support with the school librarian/media specialist. In this way, students can become familiar with what materials are available to them through the media center, while locating and selecting suitable resources for the task presented.

It is important for students to learn to use the card catalogue system, internet search engines, indexes, and other information/organizational tools. It will allow them to be able to answer their own questions throughout the remainder of their lives. They will have the necessary tools to be successful at locating any information they need.

Once the facts have been found, it is necessary for the students to have specific strategies for determining the relevance and potential usefulness of what has been gathered. No one person can manage all of the knowledge about a topic. Students need to understand this fact and learn to weed out the irrelevant information.

Graphic organizers, like outlines, may provide students with the skills to determine the relevant information. For example, though they may read about an interesting bug just found on the island about which they are studying, if insect life is not a topic on their study project outline, that information isn't important to completing the assigned task.

Determining and rating information on the basis of importance takes practice and guidance. Students who are successful with it will be most able to take the gathered information and use it to complete the assigned tasks. Because this is the end goal, it is important to demonstrate this process in a very explicit way for students to ensure success.

Guidelines for the use of secondary sources:

- Do not rely upon only a single secondary source.
- Check facts and interpretations against primary sources whenever possible.
- Accept the conclusions of other historians critically.
- Place greatest reliance on secondary sources created by the best and most respected scholars.
- Do not use the inferences of other scholars as if they were facts.
- Ensure that you recognize any bias the writer brings to his/her interpretation of history.
- Understand the primary point of the book as a basis for evaluating the value of the material presented in it to your questions.

Note Taking Skills and Outlines

Being effective note takers requires consistent technique whether the mode of note taking is on 5 X 7 note cards, lined notebook paper, or on a computer. Organizing all collected information according to a research outline will allow the user to take notes on each section and begin the writing process. If the computer is used, then the actual format of the report can be word-processed and information input to speed up the writing process of the final research report. Creating a title page and the bibliography page will allow each downloaded report to have its resources cited immediately in that section.

Note taking involves identification of specific resources that include the author's or organization's name, year of publication, title, publisher location, and publisher. Use the author's last name and page number on cited information when taking notes, whether on the computer or using note cards. In citing information for major categories and subcategories on the computer, create a file for notes that includes summaries of information and direct quotes. When direct quotes are put into a Word file, the cut-and-paste process for incorporation into the report is quick and easy.

In outline information, it is crucial to identify the headings and subheadings for the topic being researched. When researching information, it is easier to cut and paste information under the indicated headings in creating a visual flow of information for the report. In the actual drafting of the report, the writer is able to lift direct quotations and citations from the posted information to incorporate in the writing.

Mapping

Mapping is a strategy that can be used to reach all learning styles, and therefore is an important one to teach. It is exactly what its name implies—a map of the reading. A map helps the reader maneuver through the information in a meaningful manner. Maps can use words with key ideas connected to smaller chunks of information. Teachers can also encourage pictures instead of words to help the visual learner. Adding color to a map can help certain ideas stand out more. This can be particularly helpful for students to begin to understand the process of prioritization in skills. Combining words and pictures is probably the most commonly used type of map. Lines are drawn between connecting concepts to show relationships, and because the reader is creating it himself or herself, it is meaningful. Maps are individual creations and revolve around the reader's learning and prior knowledge.

Use of Text Features (e.g., Index and Glossary), Graphic Features (e.g., Charts and Maps), and Reference Materials

Traditionally, the use of expository texts has been taught in a dry format that involves reference books from the school or public library, particularly, the Atlas, Almanac, and large geography volumes.

Although these worthy books from public and classroom libraries can still be used, it is much easier to take a simple newspaper to introduce and provide children with daily, ongoing, and authentic experiences in learning these necessary skills. As an added benefit, children can keep up with real world events that affect their daily lives.

Children can go on a chronological hunt through the daily newspaper and discover the many formats of schedules printed in the paper. For instance, some newspapers include a calendar of the week with literary, sports, social, movie and other public events. Children can also go on scavenger hunts through various sections of the newspaper and, on certain days, find full-blown timelines detailing famous individuals' careers, business histories, milestones in the political history of a nation, or even key movies made by a famous movie director up for an Oscar.

Newspaper stories address the public's need to know the "why" and "wherefore" behind natural disasters, company takeovers, political downfalls, national uprisings, and the like with the support of such elements as graphic representations, cause /effect diagramming, and comparison/contrast wording. If the teacher wants to make certain that the students come away recognizing and understanding these elements, he/she can pre-clip news stories to introduce in a special NEWS center and use as "teaching" tools.

After children have been walked through these comparison/contrast news writings and cause/effect diagrams as they have appeared in the newspaper, they can be challenged to find additional examples of these text structures in the news or to rewrite familiar stories using these text structures. They can even use desktop publishing to re-author the stories using the same text structures.

If a class participates in a local Newspaper in Education program, where the classroom receives a free newspaper two to three times a week, the teacher can teach index skills. Using the index of the newspaper, children compete or cooperate in small groups to find various features.

Map and chart skills take on much more relevance and excitement when the children work on these skills using what is familiar or interesting to them—such as sports charts detailing the batting averages and pass completions of their favorite players or perhaps the box scores of their older siblings' football and baseball games. Maps dealing with holiday weather become meaningful to children as they anticipate a holiday or vacation.

Sample Test

1. A teacher gives a reading test to her third grade students to determine how well students comprehend the meaning of the text in real life situations, and examine student's reading process rather than the products of reading. What type of assessment did the teacher administer? (Skill 0001) (Rigorous)

   A DRP
   B Norm-referenced Test
   C Running Record
   D IRI

2. What is a characteristic of norm-referenced tests? (Skill 001) (Easy)

   A They measure achievement using set guidelines.
   B Children need to read them aloud.
   C Children's results are compared with others
   D They test student's basic reading skills.

3. A third grade class is taking a standardized test. One of the questions makes reference to the story, *Goodnight Moon*. A few students in the class were raised in countries other than the United States and were not exposed to this book as a child. This is an example of (Skill 0001) (Rigorous)

   A running records
   B phonemic awareness
   C reliability
   D bias

4) The purpose of a running record is to (Skill 0001) (Average)

   A record a student's oral reading on tape.
   B determine which cueing systems a child is using.
   C measure a student's comprehension level.
   D assess the child formally.

5) While a teacher is taking a running record, the student reads several words incorrectly and goes back and re-reads them correctly. This is called (Skill 0001) (Average)

   A a self-correction coded SC.
   B incorrect reading coded IR.
   C miscue analysis coded MA.
   D word insertion coded WI.

6. _____ is how well a test measures what it is supposed to measure. (Skill 0001) (Easy)

A   Reliability
B   Bias
C   Validity
D   Informal assessments

7. Work samples, reading records, surveys and checklists, and evaluation forms are all components of a(n) (Skill 0001) (Easy)

A   holistic scoring rubric.
B   portfolio assessment.
C   formal assessment.
D   informal reading inventories.

8. What should someone using a rubric to score a piece of writing holistically focus on when reviewing a piece of writing? (Skill 0001) (Average)

A   The overall structure and focus.
B   The spelling and grammar.
C   The overall neatness.
D   The creativity of the story.

9. A 1st grade teacher is listening to students whisper read at their own pace during a guided reading lesson. While working with one student, the teacher says, "Does what you just said match the letters here?". This child is most likely (Skill 0001) (Rigorous)

A   Having difficulties with comprehension.
B   Having trouble with syntax.
C   Having problems with graphophonic cues.
D   Having trouble with reading fluency.

10. What do reading conferences, reading surveys, daily reading time, and literature circles all have in common? (Skill 0001) (Rigorous)

A   They are all ways for students to offer personal responses to reading.
B   They are all ways to increase student fluency.
C   They all allow students to choose books they want to read.
D   They are all forms of guided reading.

11. When a teacher collects information about children's progress, and evaluates their reading responses this is called (Skill 0002) (Average)

A   Guided reading
B   Assessment
C   Standardized testing
D   Running record

12. A teacher keeps notes about student performance each time she meets with their guided reading group. This is an example of (Skill 0002) (Average)

A informal assessment.
B formal assessment.
C standardized testing.
D miscue analysis.

13. The characteristics of effective assessment include (Skill 0002) (Rigorous)

I.   ongoing assessment
II.   authentic assessment
III. independent reading
IV. multidimensional

A All of the above
B I, II
C II and IV
D I, II, and IV

14. Books that children can read independently are called (Skill 0002) (Easy)

A leveled readers
B "just right" books.
C instructional texts.
D emergent readers.

15. Books that support letter-sound relationships support (Skill 0002) (Average)

A comprehension
B literature response
C decodability
D oral reading

16. What is a strategy that will help children to read on their own fluently and independently? (Skill 0002) (Rigorous)

A Reading aloud with an adult to give them unknown words.
B Having a dictionary close by to look up unknown words.
C Skipping an unknown word and reading to the end of a sentence.
D Only sounding out unknown words letter by letter.

17. What is a good strategy to use to help ELL students be successful readers? (Skill 0002) (Rigorous)

A Have ELL students listen to recorded versions of stories.
B Give ELL students books that do not contain illustrations.
C Analyze story events in English only.
D Have students translate English stories into their native language.

18. Running records and miscue analysis mainly show a teacher (Skill 0002) (Average)

A how well a student can retell a story after reading.
B what the student does with their eyes while reading.
C the cueing systems a student is using while reading.
D what the student does while reading silently.

19. A Spanish speaking child enters your class half-way into the school year. It is best to build literacy experiences around (Skill 0003) (Average)

   A the student's native language.
   B the primary language of the school.
   C the ESL/ELL teacher's ideals.
   D pictures books written in English.

20. A 2nd grade student's native language is not English. While reading aloud, this student will pronounce English words that do not make sense, but keeps on reading anyway. What does the teacher need to do with this student? (Skill 0003) (Rigorous)

   A Allow them to read texts in their native language.
   B Teach the student to self-monitor and stop to construct meaning.
   C Encourage the student to substitute a word from their native language.
   D Work on phonics so the student can pronounce the word correctly.

21. Which type of listening teaches students to enjoy an experience? (Skill 0003) (Average)

   A Critical listening
   B Attentive listening
   C Passive listening
   D Appreciative listening

22. Small group discussions and brainstorming help improve students' (Skill 0003) (Easy)

   A Speaking skills only
   B Listening skills only
   C Speaking and listening skills
   D Oral reading skills

23. A teacher gives each of her 1st grade students letter cards. She then teaches a lesson which directs them in how to move the letters around to create new words. The teacher is (Skill 0003) (Average)

   A Teaching comprehension strategies.
   B Teaching the relationship between speaking and writing.
   C Performing a miscue analysis.
   D Connecting reading and math.

24. A read-aloud should (Skill 0003) (Average)

   A be at the students independent reading level.
   B always tie in the content areas.
   C always be a poetry selection
   D be interactive allowing students to offer written and oral comments.

25. The main purpose of an oral retelling of a story is to (Skill 0003) (Average)

   A Measure a student's level of comprehension.
   B Determine a students fluency rate.
   C Measure a student's vocabulary development.
   D Determine how many minute details a student can recall.

26. Sounds in spoken language working together to make words describe (Skill 0003) (Rigorous)

   A phonics.
   B phonological awareness
   C graphophonic cues
   D phonemic awareness

27. Word work, syllables, onset and rimes, and phonemes are all sub-components of (Skill 0003) (Rigorous)

   A morphology
   B phonics
   C phonological awareness
   D syntax

28. Each morning during circle time, a teacher has the students clap out the syllables in the days of the week. This activity is helping to build (Skill 0004) (Average)

   A phonemic awareness
   B rhyming
   C phonological awareness
   D auditory listening skills

29. During a guided reading lesson a teacher has the students create words with the last part –at. The teacher is building (Skill 0004) (Average)

   A graphophonic skills
   B phonemic awareness
   C word identification skills
   D phonological awareness

30. A student is whisper reading to the teacher during a guided reading lesson. The student is pronouncing the word *bend* as *blend*. What might the teacher say to help this student decode the word correctly? (Skill 0004) (Average)

   A If this were the word *blend*, what letter would it have to start with?
   B If this were the word *blend*, what letter would it have to end with?
   C If this were the word *blend*, what letter would you see after the *b*?
   D If this were the word *blend*, what vowel would you see in the word?

31. A teacher works on blending three-letter word sounds together with her kindergarten students. This activity is an example of (Skill 0004) (Easy)

A identifying rhyming sounds in words.
B identifying the number of syllables in a word.
C phonological awareness building.
D direct phonics instruction.

32. By having students explain how they were finally able to correctly decode a word that they were stuck on is an example of (Skill 0004) (Rigorous)

A metamorphosis.
B metacognition.
C phonics instruction.
D miscue analysis.

33. A monosyllabic word is (Skill 0004) (Easy)

A hard for students to recognize through clapping.
B a word with only one vowel.
C always follows the CVC pattern.
D has only one syllable.

34. One of the best ways to introduce syllabification to students is through (Skill 0004) (Average)

A repetitive flash cards.
B music and dance routines.
C poetry and shared reading.
D a guided reading lesson.

35. How does syllabification help emergent and transitional readers? (Skill 0004) (Rigorous)

A Students are able to recognize the rhythm of a story.
B Students can determine letter sounds.
C Students can decode words using syllable chunks.
D Students can easily determine prefixes and suffixes.

36. What is phonics? (Skill 0004) (Easy)

A The understanding that the sounds in spoken language make words.
B The understanding that letters represent sounds in written language.
C The understanding that words are made up of many things like syllables.
D The understanding of students reading levels and reading abilities.

37. Student-adult reading, choral reading, tape assisted reading, partner reading, and reader's theatre are all reading strategies that promote (Skill 0005) (Average)

A reading aloud
B self-monitoring
C decoding
D fluency

38. Texts that contain highly predictable elements of rhyme, sound patterns, and plot are called (Skill 0005) (Easy)

   A   decodable books.
   B   Hi-lo readers.
   C   engaging texts.
   D   whole language books

39. Choral reading is also known as (Skill 0005) (Easy)

   A   partner reading.
   B   shared reading.
   C   tape assisted reading.
   D   round robin reading.

40. A kindergarten teacher believes in doing letter and word activities only with her students before they allow their students to "read" engaging books. This teaching approach is known as (Skill 0005) (Rigorous)

   A   phonics based reading instruction.
   B   whole language reading instruction.
   C   balanced literacy reading instruction.
   D   integrated reading instruction.

41. What must be true of a systematic phonics instruction? (Skill 0006) (Average)

   A   The teacher chooses the order new information is introduced.
   B   Precise directions are included within the framework of the program.
   C   The instructional plan has a specific scope and sequence.
   D   Textbooks are used to teach specific phonics and comprehension skills.

42. What makes a phonics program *explicit?* (Skill 0006) (Easy)

   A   The teacher is given the lesson, but is not always clear on how it should be taught.
   B   Precise directions are included within the framework of the program guide.
   C   Teachers must be able to identify "teachable moments" and match it to a given lesson.
   D   It is necessary to have rich text for students to practice their new skills.

43. **A teacher has her students grouped in spelling groups by the word family they are working on this week. What type of phonics instruction is she using in her classroom? (Skill 0006) (Average)**

    A   synthetic phonics
    B   analytic phonics
    C   analogy-based phonics
    D   phonics through spelling

44. **How will systematic, explicit phonics instruction help students with their comprehension? (Skill 0006) (Rigorous)**

    A   It will allow students to become better spellers.
    B   It will allow students to recognize words more quickly.
    C   It will allow students to spend more time decoding words.
    D   It will allow students to read a great number of books quickly.

45. **When should phonics instruction begin? (Skill 0006) (Easy)**

    A   When children learn to talk.
    B   During preschool.
    C   Kindergarten or first grade.
    D   Second or third grade.

46. **Direct instruction of vocabulary words should (Skill 0007) (Average)**

    A   be done while the students are reading the text.
    B   be done after the students have read the text selection.
    C   relate to the storyline or the main idea of the selection.
    D   always be included on students spelling lists.

47. **During each guided reading lesson, how many words should a teacher introduce directly? (Skill 0007) (Average)**

    A   1-2
    B   2-3
    C   3-4
    D   4-5

48. **What is *structural analysis?* (Skill 0007) (Easy)**

    A   The process of examining how a text is organized.
    B   The process of examining meaningful word units.
    C   The process of examining how a student creates meaning.
    D   The process of examining meaningful pieces of writing.

49. **What should a primary teacher do first when introducing affixes to students? (Skill 0007) (Rigorous)**

    A Use the letter-sound correspondence format.
    B Practice the affix alone for a few days.
    C Have students read flashcards with the affix.
    D Read passages that include words with the affix.

50. **When children "sort" their words, they are participating in (Skill 0007) (Average)**

    A literacy circles.
    B structural analysis.
    C word study
    D semantic mapping

51. **Teachers who follow a more balanced literacy approach in their classrooms are most likely going to use (Skill 0007) (Average)**

    A structural analysis of new words.
    B word work embedded in mini lessons.
    C decodable books to teach vocabulary.
    D phonetic principals to teach vocabulary.

52. **What are *homographs?* (Skill 0007) (Easy)**

    A Words that have opposite meanings.
    B Words that mean the same thing.
    C Words that are spelled alike and have different meanings.
    D Words that have two or more words that sound the same.

53. **The word *irresponsible* means (Skill 0007) (Easy)**

    A not reversible
    B very responsible
    C held accountable
    D not responsible

54. **While reading, a student determines the meaning of an unknown word using the events of the story and the words and sentences around it. The student used (Skill 0007) (Average)**

    A a dictionary
    B a thesaurus
    C context clues
    D self-monitoring

55. **Understanding of the text on the surface or to what is explicitly stated is referred to as (Skill 0008) (Average)**

    A inferential comprehension.
    B literal comprehension.
    C thought-provoking comprehension.
    D internal comprehension

56. When a student is actively engaged in reading and makes judgements and decisions beyond what is stated in the text, a student is said to be using (Skill 0008) (Average)

A inferential comprehension.
B literal comprehension
C thought-provoking comprehension
D internal comprehension

57. What was the focus of reading instruction during the 1970s and 1980s? (Skill 0008) (Rigorous)

A decoding
B standardized testing
C running records
D comprehension skills

58. In the late 1970s and 1980s, Louise Rosenblatt discovered that readers are, in fact, engaged in their reading and that this aids comprehension. She also differentiated between two types of reading: *efferent* and *aesthetic.* This is known as (Skill 0008) (Average)

A the transactional approach
B comprehension skills
C asking questions
D decoding text fluently

59. What are the components of literacy as determined by Cooper in 2004? (Skill 0008) (Rigorous)

A Reading, writing and arithmetic
B Prewriting, drafting, revising, editing, and publishing
C Reading, writing, thinking, listening, viewing and discussing
D Reading, painting, creating, writing, and reviewing.

60. Some students who come from a poorer socio-economic background may be lacking in which reading comprehension skill? (Skill 0008) (Rigorous)

A scaffolding
B comprehension
C phonemic awareness
D schemata

61. What is *prosody?* (Skill 0008) (Rigorous)

A Robotic, accurate reading
B Quick reading done perfectly
C Accurate reading done quickly
D Reading with expression and inflection

62. **What should a teacher do to help improve comprehension, before students read any selection? (Skill 0009) (Rigorous)**

    A Review the week's spelling list.
    B Complete a running record.
    C Ask a literal comprehension question.
    D Give students information about what they will be reading.

63. **Prose, short stories, novels, plays and poetry are all examples of (Skill 0009) (Average)**

    A Non-fiction
    B Genres
    C Types of texts
    D Narrative genres

64. **What type of book is best suited to the beginning reader so that they can feel success in reading? (Skill 0009) (Rigorous)**

    A Wordless books
    B Predictable texts
    C Controlled vocabulary texts
    D Authentic literature

65. **What is the difference between *plot* and *story?* (Skill 0009) (Average)**

    A Story is shared by all written materials.
    B Plot is the events and actions performed by its characters.
    C Story usually develops from the conflicts.
    D Story and plot are the same thing.

66. **The series of events leading up to the turning point in a story is called (Skill 0009) (Easy)**

    A Rising action
    B Plot
    C Climax
    D Falling action

67. **Which of the following is an example of a simile? (Skill 0009) (Easy)**

    A Winter is a bear.
    B The water was refreshing.
    C The music wrapped its arms around the dancers.
    D Her smile is like a shelf of diamonds.

68. **Which of the following is an example of alliteration? (Skill 0009) (Easy)**

    A The white stripes were striking.
    B A lack of luck covered me like a black cloud.
    C Salty seawater slithered silently forward.
    D A snake hissed in the face of the enemy.

69. **Before reading a non-fiction text, what should readers do? (Skill 0010) (Average)**

A   Readers should look for a matching fiction text.
B   Readers should take a picture walk to become familiar with the story.
C   Readers should make a list of what they already know about the topic.
D   Readers should look at the organization and layout of the text.

70. **What is *semantic mapping?* (Skill 0010) (Average)**

A   A summarizing skill.
B   A way to connect known and new information.
C   A story map that uses pictures to convey ideas.
D   An after reading activity used to improve comprehension.

71. **What is *prior knowledge?* (Skill 0010) (Easy)**

A   Knowledge students already have.
B   Knowledge students gain while reading.
C   Knowledge students had but don't have anymore.
D   Knowledge students use in after reading activity

72. **A teacher is introducing a new non-fiction reading selection. She has given children a three-column chart and asked them to fill in the first column with what they know about the topic already. The teacher is using (Skill 0010) (Average)**

A   Semantic mapping
B   An after reading activity
C   A KWL chart
D   Venn diagram

73. **What is the difference between a memoir and an autobiography? (Skill 0010) (Rigorous)**

A   A memoir is shorter than an autobiography.
B   An autobiography is written by the subject.
C   A memoir is usually written in the third person.
D   A memoir is usually about one or two aspects of a person's life.

74. **An editorial is usually (Skill 0010) (Average)**

A   expresses an opinion.
B   is a compare contrast essay.
C   uses a lot of figurative language.
D   written by several different people.

75. Chronological order, logical order, and cause and effect are all (Skill 0010) (Average)

    A ways that a fictional narrative can be written.
    B books that are used with emergent readers.
    C organizational structures of non-fiction texts.
    D ways that comprehension can be taught to students.

76. Determining values, needs, constraints and demographic information are all aspects of determining a(n) (Skill 0011) (Average)

    A genre.
    B audience.
    C topic
    D writing style.

77. When writing a business letter, what is the most important aspect to pay close attention to? (Skill 0011) (Rigorous)

    A punctuation
    B jargon
    C organization
    D purpose

78. Someone lives in a neighborhood community. They write a letter to the governing board reporting that several residents on their street do not have the proper mailbox posts. They also suggest that since there is an excess of neighborhood funds in the budget, that the governing board replace these posts at their expense and then bill the homeowners. This type of writing is an example of (Skill 0011) (Average)

    A policy
    B value
    C fact
    D audience

79. When a writers emotions come across in their writing, we call this the (Skill 0011) (Easy)

    A persuasion
    B feelings
    C connotation
    D tone

80. What is the purpose of the concluding paragraph? (Skill 0011) (Average)

    A It offers a new idea that was not in the body of the piece.
    B The concluding paragraph ties together all that has been stated in the piece.
    C It needs to include the thesis sentence.
    D States the author's opinion about the topic of the essay.

81. A student states an opinion in their essay and then uses the transition word *but.* What is the relationship of the transition word to the author's opinion? (Skill 0011) (Rigorous)

   A   It shows that the to connected ideas are similar.
   B   The *but* negates what the author just stated.
   C   It shows a cause and effect relationship.
   D   The *but* gives the reader a sense of time.

82. A good transition word to use to place emphasis on an idea is (Skill 0011) (Average)

   A   of course
   B   for example
   C   recently
   D   finally

83. When it was time to leave for soccer practice, William grabbed the balls, and Corey remembered two water bottles.

   This is an example of a (Skill 0011) (Average)

   A   simple sentence
   B   independent clause
   C   transitional phrase
   D   compound/complex sentence

84. Which sentence shows the proper subject/verb agreement? (Skill 0012) (Average)

   A   Barbara, Jim, and, Kim have been looking for an apartment.
   B   Barbara, Jim, and, Kim has been looking for an apartment.
   C   Barbara, Jim, and, Kim is looking for an apartment.
   D   Barbara, Jim, and, Kim was looking for an apartment.

85. Which sentence contains the correct verb? (Skill 0012) (Easy)

   A   We choosed to paint the kitchen yellow last week.
   B   We chose to paint the kitchen yellow last week.
   C   We choose to paint the kitchen yellow last week.
   D   We chosen to paint the kitchen yellow last week.

86. What would be the correct way to rewrite the sentence, Who's hat is this? (Skill 0012) (Average)

   A   Whom's hat is this?
   B   Whom does this hat belong?
   C   Whose hat is this?
   D   Who's is this hat?

87. What skill should be taught to students who need to locate information quickly in a non-fiction selection? (Skill 0013) (Average)

A speed reading
B skimming
C text organization
D finger reading

88. Which of the following would be an example of a primary source? (Skill 0013) (Easy)

A Theoretical writings from the time.
B A book written based on hearsay.
C An article written that has used primary sources.
D A personal opinion essay about a historical figure.

89. Which genre is great for teaching cause and effect diagramming for note taking? (Skill 0013) (Average)

A narratives
B textbooks
C Internet
D newspapers

90. What is the best way to teach map and chart skills? (Skill 0013) (Average)

A Charts and maps should be meaningful to students.
B Maps and charts should be drawn by students.
C Maps and charts should come from the newspaper.
D Charts and maps should be integrated in reading comprehension.

Answer Key

1. C	46. C
2. C	47. B
3. D	48. B
4. B	49. B
5. A	50. B
6. C	51. B
7. B	52. C
8. A	53. D
9. C	54. C
10. A	55. B
11. B	56. A
12. A	57. D
13. D	58. A
14. B	59. C
15. C	60. D
16. C	61. D
17. A	62. D
18. C	63. D
19. A	64. B
20. B	65. B
21. D	66. A
22. C	67. D
23. B	68. C
24. D	69. D
25. A	70. B
26. D	71. A
27. C	72. C
28. C	73. D
29. D	74. A
30. C	75. C
31. C	76. B
32. B	77. D
33. D	78. A
34. C	79. D
35. C	80. B
36. B	81. B
37. D	82. A
38. A	83. D
39. B	84. A
40. A	85. B
41. C	86. C
42. B	87. B
43. C	88. A
44. B	89. D
45. C	90. A

Rigor Table

	Easy	Average	Rigorous
	25%	50%	25%
Question #	2, 6, 7, 14, 22, 31, 33, 36, 38, 39, 42, 45, 48, 52, 53, 66, 67, 68, 71, 79, 85, 88	4, 5, 8, 11, 12, 15, 18, 19, 21, 23, 24, 25, 28, 29, 30, 34, 37, 41, 43, 46, 47, 50, 51, 54, 55, 56, 58, 63, 65, 69, 70, 72, 74, 75, 76, 78, 80, 82, 83, 84, 86, 87, 89,90	1, 3, 9, 10, 13, 16, 17, 20, 26, 27, 32, 35, 40, 44, 49, 57, 59, 60, 61, 62, 64, 73, 77, 81

Rationales with Sample Questions

1. **A teacher gives a reading test to her third grade students to determine how well students comprehend the meaning of the text in real life situations, and examine student's reading process rather than the products of reading. What type of assessment did the teacher administer? (Skill 0001) (Rigorous)**

   A DRP
   B Norm-referenced Test
   C Running Record
   D IRI

The correct answer is C. A running record is an assessment given to students on a one-to-one basis to determine their oral reading progress. Running records are given to students in grade K-3. Running records are an important factor in determining a student's reading level. A DRP is also a reading assessment but it is used to understand how well students understand the meaning of what they read. A norm-referenced test is an assessment that measures children against one another. An IRI is a series of texts prearranged in stages of increasing difficulty.

2. **What is a characteristic of norm-referenced tests? (Skill 001) (Easy)**

   A They measure achievement using set guidelines.
   B Children need to read them aloud.
   C Children's results are compared with others
   D They test student's basic reading skills.

The correct answer is C. There are two types of tests: norm-referenced and criterion-referenced tests. Norm-referenced tests measure student results against each other. Criterion-referenced tests measure student's reading against criteria or guidelines.

3.   A third grade class is taking a standardized test. One of the questions makes reference to the story, *Goodnight Moon.* A few students in the class were raised in countries other than the United States and were not exposed to this book as a child. This is an example of (Skill 0001) (Rigorous)

    A running records
    B phonemic awareness
    C reliability
    D bias

The correct answer is D. Standardized tests are measured using three key ideas – validity, reliability, and bias. Bias in testing occurs when the information within the test or the information required to be able to respond to a multiple-choice question or constructed response is information that is not available to some test takers who come from a different cultural, ethnic, linguistic, or socioeconomic background than the majority of test takers.

4.   The purpose of a running record is to (Skill 0001) (Average)

    A record a student's oral reading on tape.
    B determine which cueing systems a child is using.
    C measure a student's comprehension level.
    D assess the child formally.

The correct answer is B. A running record is an informal assessment so choice D will not work. During a running record, teachers listen to a student read aloud and record the student's reading with symbols. Teachers then analyze their records to determine what students do while they read to help the teacher plan future instruction.

5.   While a teacher is taking a running record, the student reads several words incorrectly and goes back and re-reads them correctly. This is called (Skill 0001) (Average)

    A a self-correction coded SC.
    B incorrect reading coded IR.
    C miscue analysis coded MA.
    D word insertion coded WI.

The correct answer is A. When students go back and re-read something correctly, it shows that students are monitoring their reading. This can be assessed during a running record. The correct symbol during a running record is to draw an arrow back to where the student returns to correct, and label the arrow with an *SC.*

6. _____ is how well a test measures what it is supposed to measure. (Skill 0001) (Easy)

    A Reliability
    B Bias
    C Validity
      D   Informal assessments

The correct answer is C. Tests are measured on three levels – reliability, bias, and validity. Therefore, answer D can be dismissed at once. Reliability is the consistency of a test. Bisas may occur when there is certain background knowledge required in order to answer questions that appear on a test.

7. **Work samples, reading records, surveys and checklists, and evaluation forms are all components of a(n) (Skill 0001) (Easy)**

    A holistic scoring rubric.
    B portfolio assessment.
    C formal assessment.
    D informal reading inventories.

The answer is B. Just as a teacher puts together a portfolio to demonstrate work they have done, a portfolio of student work can be used as an assessment tool for the teacher. This is an informal method of assessment since it does not follow a standardized script.

8. **What should someone using a rubric to score a piece of writing holistically focus on when reviewing a piece of writing? (Skill 0001) (Average)**

    A The overall structure and focus.
    B The spelling and grammar.
    C The overall neatness.
    D The creativity of the story.

The correct answer is A. The purpose of a holistic rubric is to take into consideration the limited amount of time that students have to write and a well-organized, focused piece. Spelling and grammar therefore, cannot be considered in a holistic score for this reason. Since students have a limited amount of time, and do not have the opportunity to recopy, neatness cannot be considered in the score.

9. A 1st grade teacher is listening to students whisper read at their own pace during a guided reading lesson. While working with one student, the teacher says, "Does what you just said match the letters here?" This child is most likely (Skill 0001) (Rigorous)

    A Having difficulties with comprehension.
    B Having trouble with syntax.
    C Having problems with graphophonic cues.
    D Having trouble with reading fluency.

The correct answer is C. Graphophonic cues are related to the letter sound relationship of words. Students may sometimes focus on the syntax and the comprehension too carefully and ignore the letter/sound relationship all together.

10. What do reading conferences, reading surveys, daily reading time, and literature circles all have in common? (Skill 0001) (Rigorous)

    A They are all ways for students to offer personal responses to reading.
    B They are all ways to increase student fluency.
    C They all allow students to choose books they want to read.
    D They are all forms of guided reading.

The answer is A. Reading is an interactive activity. In order for students to comprehend text, they must interact with it before, during, and after reading. Therefore, the more opportunities students are given to offer their personal responses to reading, the better their comprehension will be.

11. When a teacher collects information about children's progress, and evaluates their reading responses this is called (Skill 0002) (Average)

    A Guided reading
    B Assessment
    C Standardized testing
    D Running record

The correct answer is B. Assessment should be ongoing and should be the evaluation criteria that drives instruction. Assessment should not only be used to evaluate students formally, but it should also be used to evaluate student's strengths and weaknesses.

12. **A teacher keeps notes about student performance each time she meets with their guided reading group. This is an example of (Skill 0002) (Average)**

    A informal assessment.
    B formal assessment.
    C standardized testing.
    D miscue analysis.

The answer is A. Miscue analysis is a type of informal reading assessment. However, it should not be done each time a teacher meets with a guided reading group. Therefore, the answer has to be informal assessment.

13. **The characteristics of effective assessment include (Skill 0002) (Rigorous)**

    I.   ongoing assessment
    II.   authentic assessment
    III.   independent reading
    IV.   multidimensional

    A All of the above
    B I, II
    C II and IV
    D I, II, and IV

The answer is D. Independent reading is the only item mentioned that is not a characteristic of good assessment. Assessment needs to occur often, using real students work, that examines different areas of learning.

14. **Books that children can read independently are called (Skill 0002) (Easy)**

    A leveled readers
    B "just right" books.
    C instructional texts.
    D emergent readers.

The correct answer is B. A just right book is exactly that – a book that is just right for a student to read on their own. Instructional texts are a bit more difficult for students to comprehend on their own and require the watchful eye of a teacher.

15. **Books that support letter-sound relationships support (Skill 0002) (Average)**

   A comprehension
   B literature response
   C decodability
   D oral reading

The correct answer is C. Decoding and comprehension are in fact separate reading entities. Decoding refers to the ability to word call or pronounce words correctly. Comprehension refers to what students are able to analyze or take from the text of the story.

16. **What is a strategy that will help children to read on their own fluently and independently? (Skill 0002) (Rigorous)**

   A Reading aloud with an adult to give them unknown words.
   B Having a dictionary close by to look up unknown words.
   C Skipping an unknown word and reading to the end of a sentence.
   D Only sounding out unknown words letter by letter.

The correct answer is C. Choice C is the only choice that supports best reading practices. Sounding out unknown words letter by letter is not the only strategy that readers should use. Students build fluency by developing strategies that will allow them to decode words quickly, correctly and independently.

17. **What is a good strategy to use to help ELL students be successful readers? (Skill 0002) (Rigorous)**

   A Have ELL students listen to recorded versions of stories.
   B Give ELL students books that do not contain illustrations.
   C Analyze story events in English only.
   D Have students translate English stories into their native language.

The correct answer is A. By listening to stories on tape, ELL students can follow along with a printed book. Illustrations are an important learning tool for ELL students and should be utilized often when teaching reading.

18. **Running records and miscue analysis mainly show a teacher (Skill 0002) (Average)**

   A how well a student can retell a story after reading.
   B what the student does with their eyes while reading.
   C the cueing systems a student is using while reading.
   D what the student does while reading silently.

The correct answer is C. Running record and miscue analysis are used to determine which cueing system a student is relying on the most; graphophonic, semantic or syntactic cues. This information can than be used to teach the student new and different reading strategies.

19. **A Spanish speaking child enters your class half-way into the school year. It is best to build literacy experiences around (Skill 0003) (Average)**

   A the student's native language.
   B the primary language of the school.
   C the ESL/ELL teacher's ideals.
   D pictures books written in English.

The correct answer is A. Integrating the student's native language with English will help them learn English faster. Picture books are a good resource to use, but the reading instruction is not built around them.

20. **A 2nd grade student's native language is not English. While reading aloud, this student will pronounce English words that do not make sense, but keeps on reading anyway. What does the teacher need to do with this student? (Skill 0003) (Rigorous)**

   A Allow them to read texts in their native language.
   B Teach the student to self-monitor and stop to construct meaning.
   C Encourage the student to substitute a word from their native language.
   D Work on phonics so the student can pronounce the word correctly.

The correct answer is B. Even students who speak fluent English need to learn this skill. Comprehension is interrupted if a student substitutes any word for a word they do not know. When students monitor their reading, they are listening for what makes sense and they are interacting with the text while they read.

21. **Which type of listening teaches students to enjoy an experience? (Skill 0003) (Average)**

    A Critical listening
    B Attentive listening
    C Passive listening
    D Appreciative listening

The correct answer is D. Appreciative listening occurs when we want to enjoy an experience. Critical listening occurs when we want to evaluate arguments and ideas. Attentive listening occurs when we listen to gain knowledge.

22. **Small group discussions and brainstorming help improve students' (Skill 0003) (Easy)**

    A Speaking skills only
    B Listening skills only
    C Speaking and listening skills
    D Oral reading skills

The correct answer is C. Brainstorming is a give and take of ideas from the whole group. Therefore, both speaking and listening skills are being developed.

23. **A teacher gives each of her 1ˢᵗ grade students letter cards. She then teaches a lesson which directs them in how to move the letters around to create new words. The teacher is (Skill 0003) (Average)**

    A Teaching comprehension strategies.
    B Teaching the relationship between speaking and writing.
    C Performing a miscue analysis.
    D Connecting reading and math.

The correct answer is B. Although students are not technically *writing* in this activity, they are learning the relationship between speaking and writing because the teacher is giving directions on new words that can be built or created.

24. **A read-aloud should (Skill 0003) (Average)**

    A be at the students independent reading level.
    B always tie in the content areas.
    C always be a poetry selection
    D be interactive allowing students to offer written and oral comments.

The correct answer is D. There are times when teachers read aloud to their students for pure enjoyment. However, reading comprehension requires interaction. Therefore, students should be allowed to interact with their ideas and connections about a read aloud to further enhance their comprehension.

25. **The main purpose of an oral retelling of a story is to (Skill 0003) (Average)**

    A Measure a student's level of comprehension.
    B Determine a students fluency rate.
    C Measure a student's vocabulary development.
    D Determine how many minute details a student can recall.

The correct answer is A. A good retelling of a story will usually include the main characters, the setting, the problem, and the solution. During an oral retelling, a teacher can also gather information about a student's vocabulary development. However, that is not the main purpose of asking a student to retell as story.

26. **Sounds in spoken language working together to make words, describes (Skill 0004) (Rigorous)**

    A phonics.
    B phonological awareness
    C graphophonic cues
    D phonemic awareness

The answer is D. Phonemic awareness is the understanding that the sounds in spoken language work together to make words. Phonics is the understanding that the letters represent sounds in written language. Phonological awareness includes working with words, syllables and onsets and rimes and phonemes.

27. **Word work, syllables, onset and rimes, and phonemes are all sub-components of (Skill 0004) (Rigorous)**

    A morphology
    B phonics
    C phonological awareness
    D syntax

The correct answer is C. Phonological awareness includes working with words, syllables and onsets and rimes, and phonemes. Phonics is the understanding that letters represent sounds in written language. Syntax is the grammatical correctness of the written word. And, morphology is the study of words.

28. **Each morning during circle time, a teacher has the students clap out the syllables in the days of the week. This activity is helping to build (Skill 0004) (Average)**

   A   phonemic awareness
   B   rhyming
   C   phonological awareness
   D   auditory listening skills

The correct answer is C. Although students are using their kinesthetic and auditory learning modalities, this exercise is an exercise in syllabification which is a part of phonological awareness.

29. **During a guided reading lesson a teacher has the students create words with the last part –at. The teacher is building (Skill 0004) (Average)**

   A   graphophonic skills
   B   phonemic awareness
   C   word identification skills
   D   phonological awareness

The correct answer is D. Phonological awareness is a large umbrella that encompasses word work, syllables, onsets and rimes, phonemes, rhyming, alliteration and intonation.

30. **A student is whisper reading to the teacher during a guided reading lesson. The student is pronouncing the word *bend* as *blend*. What might the teacher say to help this student decode the word correctly? (Skill 0004) (Average)**

   A   If this were the word *blend*, what letter would it have to start with?
   B   If this were the word *blend*, what letter would it have to end with?
   C   If this were the word *blend*, what letter would you see after the *b*?
   D   If this were the word *blend*, what vowel would you see in the word?

The correct answer is C. The student knows the beginning letter sound and sees the –*end* in the word. They are creating a consonant cluster *bl* that does not exist.

31. **A teacher works on blending three-letter word sounds together with her kindergarten students. This activity is an example of (Skill 0004) (Easy)**

    A identifying rhyming sounds in words.
    B identifying the number of syllables in a word.
    C phonological awareness building.
    D direct phonics instruction.

The correct answer is C. Rhyming and syllables are also part of phonological awareness, but not necessarily letter blending. Direct phonics instruction is normally program based and includes directions for the teacher.

32. **By having students explain how they were finally able to correctly decode a word that they were stuck on is an example of (Skill 0004) (Rigorous)**

    A metamorphosis.
    B metacognition.
    C phonics instruction.
    D miscue analysis.

The correct answer is B. Metacognition is thinking about your own thinking. For students to explain how they were able to decode a word, they have to think about their own thinking.

33. **A monosyllabic word is (Skill 0004) (Easy)**

    A hard for students to recognize through clapping.
    B a word with only one vowel.
    C always follows the CVC pattern.
    D has only one syllable.

The correct answer is D. A syllable is a sound portion of a word. Words can have one syllable, like the word "pig", or many syllables, like the word "congratulations" which has five syllables. The word mono means one. Therefore, a monosyllabic word has only one syllable.

34. One of the best ways to introduce syllabification to students is through (Skill 0004) (Average)

   A repetitive flash cards.
   B music and dance routines.
   C poetry and shared reading.
   D a guided reading lesson.

The correct answer is C. Poetry has a natural rhythm to it that allows students to "hear" the different syllables. Students can also clap the syllables to help solidify their understanding of the concept.

35. How does syllabification help emergent and transitional readers? (Skill 0004) (Rigorous)

   A Students are able to recognize the rhythm of a story.
   B Students can determine letter sounds.
   C Students can decode words using syllable chunks.
   D Students can easily determine prefixes and suffixes.

The correct answer is C. Knowing syllable chunks can help students decode and spell words more quickly and easily. Eventually students will be able to determine prefixes and suffixes more easily because of syllabification. But it does not help emergent and transitional readers.

36. What is phonics? (Skill 0004) (Easy)

   A The understanding that the sounds in spoken language make words.
   B The understanding that letters represent sounds in written language.
   C The understanding that words are made up of many things like syllables.
   D The understanding of students reading levels and reading abilities.

The correct answer is B. Phonics is the understanding that letters represent sounds in written language. Choice A is the definition of phonemic awareness. Choice C is part of the definition of phonological awareness.

37. **Student-adult reading, choral reading, tape assisted reading, partner reading, and reader's theatre are all reading strategies that promote (Skill 0005) (Average)**

   A reading aloud
   B self-monitoring
   C decoding
   D fluency

The correct answer is D. Fluency is the speed which students read accurately. Decoding is the early stages of fluency, but students need to decode quickly to improve their fluency.

38. **Texts that contain highly predictable elements of rhyme, sound patterns, and plot are called (Skill 0005) (Easy)**

   A decodable books.
   B Hi-lo readers.
   C engaging texts.
   D whole language books

The correct answer is A. Decodable books are perfect for emergent readers because they allow new readers to feel successful when they read. Hi-lo readers are high interest, low level readers for older readers.

39. **Choral reading is also known as (Skill 0005) (Easy)**

   A partner reading.
   B shared reading.
   C tape assisted reading.
   D round robin reading.

The correct answer is B. Choral reading and shared reading are when students read aloud as a group with the teacher. All of the other choices listed are done alone by the student or with one other student.

40. A kindergarten teacher believes in doing letter and word activities only with her students before they allow their students to "read" engaging books. This teaching approach is known as (Skill 0005) (Rigorous)

   A phonics based reading instruction.
   B whole language reading instruction.
   C balanced literacy reading instruction.
   D integrated reading instruction.

The correct answer is A. Whole language advocates believe the opposite. They believe that students learn phonics through reading engaging texts. A balanced literacy approach includes both phonics and whole language instruction.

41. What must be true of a systematic phonics instruction? (Skill 0006) (Average)

   A The teacher chooses the order new information is introduced.
   B Precise directions are included within the framework of the program.
   C The instructional plan has a specific scope and sequence.
   D Textbooks are used to teach specific phonics and comprehension skills.

The answer is C. Systematic phonics follow a very specific path of instruction. Explicit phonics instruction includes precise directions for the teacher.

42. What makes a phonics program *explicit?* (Skill 0006) (Easy)

   A The teacher is given the lesson, but is not always clear on how it should be taught.
   B Precise directions are included within the framework of the program guide.
   C Teachers must be able to identify "teachable moments" and match it to a given lesson.
   D It is necessary to have rich text for students to practice their new skills.

The answer is B. Explicit phonics instruction includes specific directions for the teacher to follow in order to teach the phonics. Systematic phonics instruction is when the instruction includes a specific scope and sequence of instruction.

43. **A teacher has her students grouped in spelling groups by the word family they are working on this week. What type of phonics instruction is she using in her classroom? (Skill 0006) (Average)**

   A synthetic phonics
   B analytic phonics
   C analogy-based phonics
   D phonics through spelling

The answer is C. Analogy-based phonics uses word families to identify unfamiliar words. Synthetic phonics is when children learn how to make letters and combinations of letters into sounds. Analytic phonics is when students do not pronounce sounds in isolation. And phonics through spelling is when students break words into phonemes.

44. **How will systematic, explicit phonics instruction help students with their comprehension? (Skill 0006) (Rigorous)**

   A It will allow students to become better spellers.
   B It will allow students to recognize words more quickly.
   C It will allow students to spend more time decoding words.
   D It will allow students to read a great number of books quickly.

The correct answer is B. Systematic, explicit phonics instruction will aid students in recognizing words more quickly. This in turn will allow students to read more books quickly.

45. **When should phonics instruction begin? (Skill 0006) (Easy)**

   A When children learn to talk.
   B During preschool.
   C Kindergarten or first grade.
   D Second or third grade.

The correct answer is C. Phonics instruction should begin in kindergarten or first grade when students are developmentally ready to grasp and learn the information presented.

46. **Direct instruction of vocabulary words should (Skill 0007) (Average)**

   A be done while the students are reading the text.
   B be done after the students have read the text selection.
   C relate to the storyline or the main idea of the selection.
   D always be included on students spelling lists.

The correct answer is C. If vocabulary words relate to the storyline or the main idea of the selection, it will help students comprehend better.

47. **During each guided reading lesson, how many words should a teacher introduce directly? (Skill 0007) (Average)**

   A 1-2
   B 2-3
   C 3-4
   D 4-5

The answer is B. Any more than 2-3 words will be too overwhelming for students and true learning will not take place.

48. **What is *structural analysis?* (Skill 0007) (Easy)**

   A The process of examining how a text is organized.
   B The process of examining meaningful word units.
   C The process of examining how a student creates meaning.
   D The process of examining meaningful pieces of writing.

The correct answer is B. Structural analysis examines meaningful word units and determines their meaning through the various word parts; affixes and root or base words.

49. **What should a primary teacher do first when introducing affixes to students? (Skill 0007) (Rigorous)**

   A Use the letter-sound correspondence format.
   B Practice the affix alone for a few days.
   C Have students read flashcards with the affix.
   D Read passages that include words with the affix.

The correct answer is B. There is a recommended sequence for introducing affixes. They include: introducing the affix in the letter-sound correspondence format, practice the affix in isolation for a few days, provide words for practice which contain the affix, move from word lists to passage reading, which includes words with the affix.

50. When children "sort" their words, they are participating in (Skill 0007) (Average)

A literacy circles.
B structural analysis.
C word creation
D semantic mapping

The correct answer is B. Literacy circles are reading groups that meet to discuss a book that a group is reading. Each member has a specific "job". Semantic mapping is a before reading activity that activates student's prior knowledge.

51. Teachers who follow a more balanced literacy approach in their classrooms are most likely going to use (Skill 0007) (Average)

A structural analysis of new words.
B word work embedded in mini lessons.
C decodable books to teach vocabulary.
D phonetic principals to teach vocabulary.

The correct answer is B. Balanced literacy teachers tend to introduce the structural components as part of mini lessons that are focused on the student's reading and writing. Other teachers who choose to directly teach structural analysis, are teachers that teach following the phonics-centered approach.

52. What are *homographs*? (Skill 0007) (Easy)

A Words that have opposite meanings.
B Words that mean the same thing.
C Words that are spelled alike and have different meanings.
D Words that have two or more words that sound the same.

The correct answer is C. Some examples of homographs are lie, tear, bow, fair, bass. Homophones are words like sea – see; there, their, they're; meat – meet. These words are spelled differently but are pronounced the same way.

53. The word *irresponsible* means (Skill 0007) (Easy)

A not reversable
B very responsible
C held accountable
D not responsible

The correct answer is D. To determine the meaning of the word *irresponsible*, it is helpful to know that the prefix *ir-* means *not*. Therefore, the word *irresponsible* means *not responsible.*

54. **While reading, a student determines the meaning of an unknown word using the events of the story and the words and sentences around it. The student used (Skill 0007) (Average)**

   A   a dictionary
   B   a thesaurus
   C   context clues
   D   self-monitoring

The answer is C. Context clues are clues we gather from reading to help us understand what an unknown word means. A dictionary will also serve this purpose. But, when was the last time you stopped reading a story to go and look up an unknown word in the dictionary and then continued with your reading. Readers do not do this and therefore, need to rely on the context clues.

55. **Understanding of the text on the surface or to what is explicitly stated is referred to as (Skill 0008) (Average)**

   A   inferential comprehension.
   B   literal comprehension.
   C   thought-provoking comprehension.
   D   internal comprehension

The answer is B. Literal comprehension questions usually begin with when, or where and their answers can be found within the text. Inferential questions are often thought of as "author and me" questions because the reader needs to use what they author has told them along with their own background knowledge to come up with the correct answer.

56. **When a student is actively engaged in reading and makes judgements and decisions beyond what is stated in the text, a student is said to be using (Skill 0008) (Average)**

   A   inferential comprehension.
   B   literal comprehension
   C   thought-provoking comprehension
   D   internal comprehension

The answer is A. Inferential comprehension requires a student to "think". Answers are not explicitly stated within the text and the reader needs to rely on their background knowledge to make judgments and decisions about the text.

57. **What was the focus of reading instruction during the 1970s and 1980s? (Skill 0008) (Rigorous)**

    A decoding
    B standardized testing
    C running records
    D comprehension skills

The answer is D. Students during this time period came away with knowledge of how to determine: the main idea, sequence, cause and effect and other comprehension strategies. Prior to this time period, during the 60s and early 70s, teachers focused on decoding. However, we now realize that this is simply word calling and does not force readers to be actively engaged with the text.

58. **In the late 1970s and 1980s, Louise Rosenblatt discovered that readers are, in fact, engaged in their reading and that this aids comprehension. She also differentiated between two types of reading: *efferent* and *aesthetic*. This is known as (Skill 0008) (Average)**

    A the transactional approach
    B comprehension skills
    C asking questions
    D decoding text fluently

The answer is A. Louise Rosenblatt said that reading is a transaction between the reader and the text. Efferent reading is looking for and remembering information to use functionally such as filling out a job application, or reading in preparation for a test. Aesthetic reading is reading for pleasure or to make persona connections with the text.

59. **What are the components of literacy as determined by Cooper in 2004? (Skill 0008) (Rigorous)**

    A Reading, writing and arithmetic
    B Prewriting, drafting, revising, editing, and publishing
    C Reading, writing, thinking, listening, viewing and discussing
    D Reading, painting, creating, writing, and reviewing.

The correct answer is C. In order to be literate, one must engage in reading, writing, thinking, listening, viewing and discussing. Choice B are the stages of the writing process.

60. **Some students who come from a poorer socio-economic background may be lacking in which reading comprehension skill? (Skill 0008) (Rigorous)**

    A scaffolding
    B comprehension
    C phonemic awareness
    D schemata

The correct answer is D. Schemata are structures that represent generic concepts stored in our memory. Young children develop their schemata through experiences. It is the teacher's responsibility to scaffold any missing information for students who may be lacking in their background knowledge or schemata.

61. **What is *prosody? (*Skill 0008) (Rigorous)**

    A Robotic, accurate reading
    B Quick reading done perfectly
    C Accurate reading done quickly
    D Reading with expression and inflection

The correct answer is D. Students who read with prosody pay attention to punctuation and use it to clue their reading. They read with expression, appropriate phrasing, and good inflection. It may not be perfect reading, but it will sound nice and will be easy to follow as a listener.

62. **What should a teacher do to help improve comprehension, before students read any selection? (Skill 0009) (Rigorous)**

    A Review the week's spelling list.
    B Complete a running record.
    C Ask a literal comprehension question.
    D Give students information about what they will be reading.

The correct answer is D. When teachers give students information about what they will be reading, or elicit information from the students about what they will be reading, the teacher is scaffolding any missing information in children's schemata. This puts all children at the same advantage before reading the text.

63. **Prose, short stories, novels, plays and poetry are all examples of (Skill 0009) (Average)**

    A Non-fiction
    B Genres
    C Types of texts
    D Narrative genres

The correct answer is D. All of the above examples are of narratives. Narratives usually have characters, a setting, a central problem, and a solution. They are normally not written to teach information.

64. **What type of book is best suited to the beginning reader so that they can feel success in reading? (Skill 0009) (Rigorous)**

    A Wordless books
    B Predictable texts
    C Controlled vocabulary texts
    D Authentic literature

The correct answer is B. Predictable books present a word pattern that is repeated from page to page changing usually one word each time. This allows emergent readers to rely on picture clues, and beginning word sounds to decode one word at a time. Controlled vocabulary texts may be boring and not allow the child to feel successful.

65. **What is the difference between *plot* and *story*? (Skill 0009) (Average)**

    A Story is shared by all written materials.
    B Plot is the events and actions performed by its characters.
    C Story usually develops from the conflicts.
    D Story and plot are the same thing.

The correct answer is B. Plot is the events and actions in the narrative perfomed by its charaters. Story is a synopsis of the temporal order of what happens in a narrative.

66. **The series of events leading up to the turning point in a story is called (Skill 0009) (Easy)**

    A Rising action
    B Plot
    C Climax
    D Falling action

The correct answer is A. The clue here is "leading up to" which is the same as rising. The climax is the pinnacle of the story where it reaches its peak. Falling action leads us down to the conclusion of the story.

67. **Which of the following is an example of a simile? (Skill 0009) (Easy)**

    A Winter is a bear.
    B The water was refreshing.
    C The music wrapped its arms around the dancers.
    D Her smile is like a shelf of diamonds.

The correct answer is D. A simile uses the words like or as to compare two or more things. A metaphor compares without using these words as in choice A. Choice C is an example of personification.

68. **Which of the following is an example of alliteration? (Skill 0009) (Easy)**

    A The white stripes were striking.
    B A lack of luck covered me like a black cloud.
    C Salty seawater slithered silently forward.
    D A snake hissed in the face of the enemy.

The answer is C. Alliteration occurs when the first sound of words is repeated as in: Salty seawater slithered silently. The consonant "s" is repeated four times. Choice a is an example of assonance and choice B is an example of consonance. Choice D uses onomatopoeia.

69. **Before reading a non-fiction text, what should readers do? (Skill 0010) (Average)**

    A Readers should look for a matching fiction text.
    B Readers should take a picture walk to become familiar with the story.
    C Readers should make a list of what they already know about the topic.
    D Readers should look at the organization and layout of the text.

The correct answer is D. Non-fiction is organized in many different ways. By previewing how a text is organized, readers can make a plan of how they want to go about gaining the information presented in the non-fiction text. Some teachers may ask students, as a before reading activity, to make a list of what they already know about a topic. However, this is normally not done by a reader's independent choice.

70. **What is *semantic mapping*? (Skill 0010) (Average)**

    A A summarizing skill.
    B A way to connect known and new information.
    C A story map that uses pictures to convey ideas.
    D An after reading activity used to improve comprehension.

The answer is B. Semantic mapping usually takes place before reading and is done to bring student's background or prior knowledge about a topic to the forefront so that they are ready to read a selection about the topic. It is also used by the teacher as a way to scaffold information for children who may not have any information about a topic in their schemata.

71. **What is *prior knowledge*? (Skill 0010) (Easy)**

    A Knowledge students already have.
    B Knowledge students gain while reading.
    C Knowledge students had but don't have anymore.
    D Knowledge students use in after reading activity.

The answer is A. Another word for prior knowledge is background knowledge. It is the knowledge that students already have. It is important for student's comprehension to activate their background knowledge before reading.

72. **A teacher is introducing a new non-fiction reading selection. She has given children a three-column chart and asked them to fill in the first column with what they know about the topic already. The teacher is using (Skill 0010) (Average)**

    A Semantic mapping
    B An after reading activity
    C A KWL chart
    D Venn diagram

The correct answer is C. A KWL chart organizes what students know about a topic, what they want to know about a topic and what they learned about a topic after reading.

73. **What is the difference between a memoir and an autobiography? (Skill 0010) (Rigorous)**

    A A memoir is shorter than an autobiography.
    B An autobiography is written by the subject.
    C A memoir is usually written in the third person.
    D A memoir is usually about one or two aspects of a person's life.

The correct answer is D. An autobiography is an account of a person's life written by that person. A memoir is a type of autobiography, but usually deals with only one or two aspects of the author's life. It is not as structured as an autobiography because of this.

74. **An editorial is usually (Skill 0010) (Average)**

    A expresses an opinion.
    B is a compare contrast essay.
    C uses a lot of figurative language.
    D written by several different people.

The correct answer is A. An editorial is a statement or a news article written by a news organization. It normally does not use any figurative language and is written by one person.

75. **Chronological order, logical order, and cause and effect are all (Skill 0010) (Average)**

    A ways that a fictional narrative can be written.
    B books that are used with emergent readers.
    C organizational structures of non-fiction texts.
    D ways that comprehension can be taught to students.

The correct answer is C. Chronological order is a listing of events as they happen from beginning to end. Logical order is the physical order of the text and differs according to topic. Cause and effect is a type of informational text discussing the topic in terms of what causes it or what it causes and the effect this has on other objects or people.

76. **Determining values, needs, constraints and demographic information are all aspects of determining a(n) (Skill 0011) (Average)**

    A genre.
    B audience.
    C topic
    D writing style.

The answer is B. The audience is the people that a piece of writing is written for. Depending on the audience values, needs, constraints and demographic information determines how the piece will be written.

77. **When writing a business letter, what is the most important aspect to pay close attention to? (Skill 0011) (Rigorous)**

    A punctuation
    B jargon
    C organization
    D purpose

The answer is D. A business letter is written to achieve something specific. Therefore, the most important aspect to pay close attention to is the purpose of the letter.

78. Someone lives in a neighborhood community. They write a letter to the governing board reporting that several residents on their street do not have the proper mailbox posts. They also suggest that since there is an excess of neighborhood funds in the budget, that the governing board replace these posts at their expense and then bill the homeowners. This type of writing is an example of (Skill 0011) (Average)

A policy
B value
C fact
D audience

The answer is A. Policy is a type of persuasive speech that calls one to action. It argues that something should be done, improved, or changed. Its goal is action from the audience, but it also seeks passive agreement with the proposition proposed. It also offers a solution or suggestion.

79. When a writers emotions come across in their writing, we call this the (Skill 0011) (Easy)

A persuasion
B feelings
C connotation
D tone

The correct answer is D. The emotions or attitude that a writer might portray in their writing may be playful, formal, intimate, angry, serious, ironic, outraged, baffled, tender, serene, or depressed to name a few.

80. What is the purpose of the concluding paragraph? (Skill 0011) (Average)

A It offers a new idea that was not in the body of the piece.
B The concluding paragraph ties together all that has been stated in the piece.
C It needs to include the thesis sentence.
D States the author's opinion about the topic of the essay.

The answer is B. The concluding paragraph's purpose is to tie the ideas presented in the piece together. It is not the place to introduce a new idea into the piece. It may restate the thesis sentence but it is not a requirement. It may also include the author's opinion, but this is not the main purpose of the concluding paragraph.

81. **A student states an opinion in her essay and then uses the transition word *but*. What is the relationship of the transition word to the author's opinion? (Skill 0011) (Rigorous)**

A It shows that the two connected ideas are similar.
B The *but* negates what the author just stated.
C It shows a cause and effect relationship.
D The *but* gives the reader a sense of time.

The answer is B. Anytime the word but is used, it negates what preceded it. For example, "It is a beautiful day today, but there are a lot of bugs out".

82. **A good transition word to use to place emphasis on an idea is (Skill 0011) (Average)**

A of course
B for example
C recently
D finally

The correct answer is A. Breakfast is the most important meal of the day. Of course, it is important to eat something substantial. The use of the transition *of course* places emphasis on the fact that breakfast is the most important meal of the day.

83. **When it was time to leave for soccer practice, William grabbed the balls, and Corey remembered two water bottles.**

This is an example of a (Skill 0011) (Average)

A simple sentence
B independent clause
C transitional phrase
D compound/complex sentence

The answer is D. A simple sentence has one independent clause. A compound sentence consists of two or more independent clauses. A complex sentence consists of an independent clause plus one or more dependent clauses. A compound complex sentence consists of one or more dependent clauses plus two or more independent clauses – which is what makes up the sentence in the example.

84. **Which sentence shows the proper subject/verb agreement? (Skill 0012) (Average)**

   A Barbara, Jim, and, Kim have been looking for an apartment.
   B Barbara, Jim, and, Kim has been looking for an apartment.
   C Barbara, Jim, and, Kim is looking for an apartment.
   D Barbara, Jim, and, Kim was looking for an apartment.

The answer is A. The verb *have* is used here because there are multiple people as the subject. Has and is are used to support a single subject. *Was looking* happened in the past and the correct verb would be *were*.

85. **Which sentence contains the correct verb? (Skill 0012) (Easy)**

   A We choosed to paint the kitchen yellow last week.
   B We chose to paint the kitchen yellow last week.
   C We choose to paint the kitchen yellow last week.
   D We chosen to paint the kitchen yellow last week.

The answer is B. Chose is the correct past tense form of the verb *to choose*.

86. **What would be the correct way to rewrite the sentence, Who's hat is this? (Skill 0012) (Average)**

   A Whom's hat is this?
   B Whom does this hat belong?
   C Whose hat is this?
   D Who's is this hat?

The correct answer is C. The way the sentence is written now actually could read, "Who is hat is this?" and that does not make sense grammatically. The correct way to write this would be *whose*.

87. **What skill should be taught to students who need to locate information quickly in a non-fiction selection? (Skill 0013) (Average)**

   A speed reading
   B skimming
   C text organization
   D finger reading

The answer is B. Skimming is a valuable skill for students to know in order to locate information quickly.

88. **Which of the following would be an example of a primary source? (Skill 0013) (Easy)**

    A   Theoretical writings from the time.
    B   A book written based on hearsay.
    C   An article written that has used primary sources.
    D   A personal opinion essay about a historical figure.

The answer is A. Primary sources are works, records, etc. that were created during the period being studied or immediately after it. Secondary sources are works written significantly after the period being studied and are based upon primary sources.

89. **Which genre is great for teaching cause and effect diagramming for note taking? (Skill 0013) (Average)**

    A   narratives
    B   textbooks
    C   Internet
    D   newspapers

The correct answer is D. Newspapers are great for teaching cause and effect because news stories address the public's need to know including the why and wherefore about our world.

90. **What is the best way to teach map and chart skills? (Skill 0013) (Average)**

    A   Charts and maps should be meaningful to students.
    B   Maps and charts should be drawn by students.
    C   Maps and charts should come from the newspaper.
    D   Charts and maps should be integrated in reading comprehension.

The correct answer is A. Maps and charts are much more exciting, captivating and interesting when they are familiar to them. Good examples are sports charts about batting averages, pass completions or student's own sporting event statistics. Another good type of chart is a weather chart about an upcoming holiday.

CONSTRUCTED RESPONSE PROBLEMS

Constructed Response I

Jean is a first-year teacher who is taking over the classroom of a thirty-year veteran teacher who is retiring. Jean goes in to meet with the teacher. The teacher, Ms. Banks, talks about the importance of teaching the young first graders the *concepts of print*.

She gives Jean a list of these concepts and suggests that Jean create some assessment format so that she can be certain that all of her first graders learn these concepts. She also tells Jean that she will be volunteering her time in a neighborhood preschool program close to her home and so she will be taking her private books and materials with her. She suggests that Jean go over the list of *concepts of print* and consider the needs of her class as she prepares for teaching this crucial set of skills.

Ms. Banks' list of *concepts of print* includes:

- STARTS ON LEFT

- GOES FROM LEFT TO RIGHT

- RETURN SWEEP

- MATCHES WORDS BY POINTING

- POINTS TO JUST ONE WORD

- POINTS TO FIRST AND LAST WORD

- POINTS TO ONE LETTER

- POINTS TO FIRST AND LAST LETTER

- PARTS of the BOOK: Cover, Title Page, Dedication Page, Author, and Illustrator

Jean thanks Ms. Banks for all of this help and asks if she can send Ms. Banks some of her teaching ideas for *Concepts of Print*. Ms. Banks smiles and says she feels good to know that her classroom will be taken over by Jean. She promises to review Jean's response.

Constructed Response Problem One: Answer

First, as far as assessment for the key skills of *concepts of print,* I have decided that it is very important that I have a record of when and how well each of my students masters these concepts. After much thought, I realized that I will be keeping assessment notebooks for all of my students as part of my general reading and teaching. Therefore, I plan to print out all the key *concepts of print* on an 8" x 11" piece of paper in a grid format. This sheet will be included with other assessment grids for each individual child.

After I conference with the child and determine the child has demonstrated mastery of a particular concept, I will check it off on the grid and date that mastery. If I have other comments to make about the child's level of mastery or fluency, I will make an anecdotal notation about the child as well. I think that this will guarantee that I have a detailed checklist record and anecdotal record of individual progress on *concepts of print* for the children in my class.

I plan to use big books and many of the latest picture books, including Caldecott award winners in demonstrating and sharing with children many of the *concepts of print.* I will do much of my instruction mini-lessons. In fact I intend to use some of my own favorite alphabet books to introduce these conventions. With a book like Clare Beaton's *Zoe and Her Zebra*, I can easily and naturally cover the title page, cover, illustrator, and also manage to engage the children in the use of repetitive language.

Once I have shared that delightful book with the children as a read-aloud, we will be able to return to it again and use the repetitive language in it in its big-book format to demonstrate for the children how they can point under each word as if there is a button to push. I can also demonstrate for the children how they should start at the top of the text and move from left to right. I will model going back to the left and under the previous line in a return sweep.

After modeling this as part of the mini-lesson, the children can be divided in small groups or pairs to take other big books and practice the "point under each word" and the "return sweep" as part of "shared reading" or buddy reading. I will ask that these "buddies" take time in small groups to work on another book from the alphabet book collection to share with the class as a whole. The use of the alphabet books also helps me to get some time in on the alphabetic principle.

I will also do a classroom writing workshop using the original alphabet book I use for the read-aloud, say *Zoe and Her Zebra* as a model for creating our own story. Perhaps we will call it *Barry and His Boxer*. In this way, we will have a concrete literary product that demonstrates the children's mastery of and fluency in the *concepts of print* as they create an "in-the-style-of" story about a peer using illustrations, title page, dedication page, numbering of pages, back and front cover, and other *concepts of print.*

I think that using individualized assessments, a group/class collaborative writing project, and an anchor alphabet book, will help me successfully teach the *concepts of print*.

Constructed Response II

Margaret, a new fist grade teacher, is told by her principal that her new class has three children who are from ELL backgrounds where their families are not involved in oral story telling or reading from native language texts. The principal has asked that Margaret submit a written plan to her detailing how Margaret intends to differentiate instruction for the ELL children in her classroom. What should Margaret's response look like?

Constructed Response Problem Two: Answer

Through the use of formal and informal assessments, I will be able to identify some highly proficient readers who will be happy to serve as "buddy" reader/tutors for the ELL children. Monday through Thursday proficient readers will read with their ELL student buddy. On Friday, the ELL students can read the "buddy" book independently.

In addition to buddy reading daily, ELL students will rotate through various literacy centers that include books on tape, writing stories about various illustrations using both English and their native language, and re-reading predictable, familiar books. These activities will acclimate students to the English language and help build their own sense of story which is lacking in their background knowledge.

ELL students will also be exposed to phonics daily through the use of a systematic, explicit phonics program administered by the teacher daily for approximately 5-10 minutes. In addition, I will integrate phonological awareness activities such as rhyming, syllable work and identifying onsets and rimes. These activities can be integrated into language arts mini-lessons and benefit all students in the class including ELL students. The phonological awareness activities will help ELL students identify individual phonemes and their coordinating sounds to improve their reading and their English language skills.

Additionally, ELL students will be given many opportunities to practice speaking using the English language. They will do this through class participation in the various content areas, retelling of books they have read in guided reading groups, read alouds, or independently. By integrating all of these reading, writing, speaking and listening activities, it is expected that the ELL student's growth in English language and literacy will be great and swift.

Constructed Response Problem III

Marianne has been selected as one of a team of teachers who will start teaching in a brand new school building that has been under construction for several years. While Marianne, a grade three teacher, is thrilled to be moving into new facilities, she is a bit overwhelmed to have to "set up her room" all over again at the new site. Her administrator, Mr. Adams, tells her that there are five new teachers, with no previous experience teaching primary school-age children, who will be on staff. He tells her that these educators could really use help setting up their classrooms.

Marianne smiles and decides that she would very much like to use her set-up of her own grade three classroom as a workshop and demonstration for setting up a literacy teaching environment for these new staff members. Mr. Adams thinks that is a great idea and asks Marianne for an agenda and for a general description of what she will cover in her three-hour workshop so that he can give it to the district office.

Marianne is happy to comply because she realizes that she will be assisting new colleagues and getting 10 helping hands to help her set up all the materials she has accumulated over a 20-year career.

Constructed Response Problem Three: Answer

The concept of sharing with new colleagues how to set up a classroom is very exciting to me. I know, based on my experiences, how crucial a well-planned and conceptualized space is for young learners' literacy learning. Therefore, this is an agenda for what I will cover in my three-hour in-service session with my new colleagues.

First, I will discuss how whatever the size of the classroom space, it must be sectioned off into the following areas: a meeting area, with a sofa or "soft" setting; a chair, easel, and basket to store book bags; a conference table; children's tables; a bin/basket main area for trade books; and another space for computers.

I may even give out a diagram of my classroom from my old school and some pictures. We will discuss collaboratively how I will set up my own new space as well as how they will want to set up their own spaces to allow for different uses of space within their own classrooms.

I will get into the issue of whether or not they want to have a traditional desk for each student or use small tables for everyone. I think that they will need time to consider their own teaching styles in this regard. All teachers need to set up a space where they can easily confer with children and have access to individual assessment notebooks; reading folders; and poetry/spelling, reading response, and handwriting notebooks for all their students. I intend to show them how to prepare these folders for each child and how to store them so they can get to them when they need to make additional annotations for each child. Given the fact that I am working with new colleagues, I suspect that this will take at least an hour and a half of our time. I am also going to model for them a weekly reading log.

Most important of all, I am going to spend the major amount of time talking to them about the book bins as I place mine around the classroom. I will show them how to label the books using the Fountas and Pinnell levels and how to arrange the book bins with the spines out so that the children can see the books.

Together we will examine how the bookcases should be close to the walls and the expository books should be separated from the narrative texts. I will also get together my audio-cassettes and book sets so that they can see how I set up my read-along center for all my children. I will share some dual language tapes I use with ELL students as well. I have some extra "author's hats" and author's chair slipcovers I will share with them.

I also intend to show them how to select big books for the easel display and anchor books to be shown there as well. By the way, I will also coach them how to write away for supplies and how to store supplies in common areas so that some children are not missing necessary materials for class activities.
Even though we are focusing on literacy, I am going to show them where to store mathematics materials, other texts, and art supplies. I will end the session by making sure that they know where to place their *chart wall* and the *word wall*. If I have time, I will sit down with each of them and start them on the *word wall* and some key charts for their first day. They will leave my room with an actual experience of setting up a literacy environment, plus viable teaching and reading suggestions for the first day. Most importantly, I will be available for an in-school classroom consultation, if necessary.

Constructed Response Problem IV

Write and essay answering the prompt:
A problem people recognize and should do something about.

In your essay, show your understanding of writing skills and the processes used to create a coherent, cohesive essay.

Constructed Response Problem Four: Answer

Sample Strong Response

Time magazine, which typically selects a person of the year, chose Earth as the planet of the year in 1988 to underscore the severe problems facing our planet and therefore us. We hear dismal reports everyday about the water shortage, the ozone depletion, and the obscene volume of trash generated by our society. Because the problem is global, many people feel powerless to help. Fortunately, by being environmentally aware, we can take steps to alter what seems inevitable. We can recycle our trash and support politicians and lobbying groups who will work for laws to protect the environment.

While one day recycling may be mandatory in all states, right now it is voluntary in many communities. Those of us who participate in recycling are amazed by how much material is recycled. For many communities, the blue box recycling program has had an immediate effect. by just recycling glass, aluminum cans, and plastic bottles, we have reduced the volume of disposable trash by one-third, thus extending the useful life of local landfills by over a decade. Imagine the difference if those dramatic results were achieved nationwide. The amount of reusable items we thoughtlessly dispose of is staggering. For example, Americans dispose of enough steep everyday to supply Detroit car manufacturers for three months. Additionally, we dispose of enough aluminum annually to rebuild the nation's air fleet. These statistics, available from the Environmental Protection Agency (EPA) should encourage us to watch what we throw away. Clearly, recycling in our homes and communities directly improves the environment.

Moreover, we must be aware of the political issues involved in environmental protection because, unfortunately, the environmental crisis continues despite policies and laws on the books. Enacted in the 1970s, the federal Clean Water Act was intended to clean up polluted waters through the nation and to provide safe drinking water for everyone. However, today, with the Water Act still in place, dangerous medical waste has washed onto public beaches in Florida and recently several people died from the polluted drinking water in Madison Wisconsin. Additionally, contradictory government policies often work against resource protection. For example, some state welfare agencies give new mothers money only for disposable, not cloth, diapers. In fact, consumer groups found that cloth diapers are cheaper initially and save money over time as we struggle with the crisis of bulging landfills. Clearly, we need consistent government policies and stiffer laws to ensure mandatory enforcement and heavy fines for polluters. We can do this best by electing politicians who will fight for such laws and voting out those who won't.

We can also work to save our planet by supporting organizations that lobby for meaningful, enforceable legal changes. Most of us do not have time to write letters, send telegrams, or study every issue concerning the environment. We can join several organizations that act as watchdogs for us all. For example, organizations such as Greenpeace, the Cousteau Society and the Sierra Club all offer memberships for as low as 15 dollars. By supporting these organizations, we ensure that they have the necessary resources to keep working for all of us and do not have to alter their standards because they must accept funding from special interest groups.

Clearly, we all must become environmentally aware. Only through increase awareness can we avoid the tragic consequences of living on a dying planet. We must actively support recycling programs and support those who fight to protect our fragile environment.

Analysis: While not every essay needs to be this thorough in order to pass the exam, this essay shows that with a clear thesis and concept in mind, a writer can produce a literate, interesting piece at one sitting. The introduction creates interest in the general topic and leads to a thesis in the last sentence. The reader has a very clear idea what will be addressed in the essay, and all body paragraphs have topic sentences that relate to the thesis and provide transition. The numerous supporting details and examples are presented in the sophisticated style that reads easily and is enhanced by a college-level vocabulary and word choice. Transition words and phrases add unity to sentences and paragraphs. Grammar and mechanics areas are correct, so errors don't detract from the fine writing. For all these reasons, this essay is a polished piece of writing deserving of an upper-range score.

XAMonline, Inc.
25 First Street, Suite 106
Cambridge, MA 02141
P: 1-800-509-4128
F: 617-583-5552

www.XAMonline.com

2010

VA VCLA, VRA and PRAXIS

PO#:	Store/School:			
Address 1:				
Address 2:				
City, State, Zip:				
Credit Card #:			Exp:	
Phone			Fax:	
Email				

ISBN	TITLE	Qty	Retail	Total
978-1-60787-059-3	Middle School Science 0439		$59.95	
978-1-60787-058-6	ESOL - English to Speakers of Other Languages 0360		$34.95	
978-1-60787-053-1	French Sample Test 0173		$15.00	
978-1-60787-047-0	Physics 0265		$59.95	
978-1-60787-046-3	Earth and Space Sciences 20571		$59.95	
978-1-60787-043-2	Art Sample Test 10133		$19.95	
978-1-60787-041-8	Educational Leadership 0410		$59.95	
978-1-60787-040-1	Physical Education 10091		$59.95	
978-1-60787-039-5	Library Media Specialist 0310		$59.95	
978-1-60787-037-1	Special Education: Teaching Students with Behavioral Disorders/Emotional Disturbance 0371		$21.95	
978-1-60787-035-7	Early Childhood 020, 022		$59.95	
978-1-60787-034-0	Reading 0200, 0201, 0202		$59.95	
978-1-60787-032-6	School Guidance & Counseling 20420		$59.95	
978-1-60787-031-9	Biology 20231, 20232, 20235		$59.95	
978-1-58197-718-9	Spanish 10191, 30194		$59.95	
978-1-58197-691-5	Chemistry 20241 20242, 20245		$59.95	
978-1-58197-269-6	Middle School English Language Arts 10049		$59.95	
978-1-58197-268-9	General Science 10435		$59.95	
978-1-58197-263-4	Middle School Social Studies 0089		$59.95	
978-1-58197-054-8	Government/Poltical Science 10930		$59.95	
available in April	Middle School Mathematics 0069		*	
available in April	Special Education: Knowledge-Based Core Principles 0351		*	
available in April	Education of Exceptional Students: Core Content Knowledge		*	
available in April	Elementary Education 0011, 0012		*	
available in April	Elementary Educatoin 0014, 0012		*	
available in April	English Language, Literature, and Composition 0041		*	
available in April	Fundamental Subjects 0511		*	
available in April	Mathematics 0061		*	
available in April	ParaPro Assessment 0755		*	
available in April	PPST I: Basic Skills 0710, 0720, 0730		*	
available in April	Principals of Learning and Teaching 0522		*	
available in April	Principals of Learning and Teaching 0524		*	
available in April	Social Studies 0081		*	
978-1-60787-108-8	VCLA Virginia Communication and Literacy Assessment		$59.95	
978-1-60787-109-5	VRA 001 Reading Assessment for Elementary and Special Education Teachers		$59.95	
			SUBTOTAL	
	1 book $8.70, 2 books $11.00. 3+ books $15.00		Ship	
			TOTAL	

CPSIA information can be obtained at www.ICGtesting.com
Printed in the USA
BVOW021001290113

311858BV00003B/135/P